8/10

FINDING, TRAINING, AND KEEPING GREAT SERVICE EMPLOYEES 101

RICHARD D. OLLEK, CBSE

authorHOUSE®

AuthorHouse™
1663 Liberty Drive
Bloomington, IN 47403
www.authorhouse.com
Phone: 1-800-839-8640

First published by AuthorHouse 6/5/2009

ISBN: 978-1-4389-9073-6 (e)
ISBN: 978-1-4389-8986-0 (sc)
ISBN: 978-1-4389-8987-7 (hc)

Library of Congress Control Number: 2009905697

Printed in the United States of America
Bloomington, Indiana

This book is printed on acid-free paper.

DEDICATED TO

My daughter, Robyn, who did all the HARD work on this book. In addition to being my wonderful daughter, she has been my Administrative Assistant for over 20 years (she started young). Whenever I have needed assistance on ANY project such as how to turn on a computer, she has always been there---day, night, weekends, holidays---anytime. Robyn, what would I do without you? YOUR MOTHER AND I LOVE YOU VERY MUCH.

CONTENTS

ACKNOWLEDGMENTS

First and most important, I give praise, glory, honor, and thanks to my risen Savior, Jesus Christ, who continues to bless my life each and every day. His saving grace brings total peace and comfort to my life every day.

I want to thank my loving wife Barbara who inspires my every day with her love, support and encouragement. I am the luckiest guy alive.

And last but not least, Caesar, my Boston Terrier who was by my side every day as this was written. His esteemed opinion and approval was sought on everything written in this book. Woof! Woof!

DISCLAIMER

Neither the author or its legal counsel make any representations as to the legality of the ideas or statements contained in this book. They represent the ideas and opinions of the author only, and in no way provide a guarantee of success for the reader, as every company and individual situation will be different as will the commitment to any program or process. Furthermore, any cost estimates or prices are based on information deemed reliable but not guaranteed and are used for the purposes of illustration only. All persons should consult with their own legal and financial counsel concerning the many questions and issues that may arise. Furthermore, neither the author nor its legal counsel make any claims as to the overall professionalism of any companies mentioned in this book.

INTRODUCTION

What you will read in this book is a compilation of over 46 years in the Building Service Contracting industry. There are no sophisticated studies that espouse complicated theories. There are only my personal experiences, observations, stories, and thoughts on what I consider to be key ingredients to being successful in finding and keeping GREAT service employees.

You will not read of sophisticated or laboratory studies done regarding what works or doesn't work in the service industry. You will only read of my thoughts and experiences of procedures and policies that have worked.

I've never been too good on theory. All I know is what I have experienced in the 46 plus years in the service business, 37 of them being a business owner.

What qualifies me to write this book? That's easy---lots of mistakes. They say we learn from our mistakes. If that is in fact true, I should be one of the most knowledgeable people on this subject of Human Resources. I certainly have the battle scars to prove it. I am hoping by your reading this compilation of my thoughts you can avoid many of the mistakes that can cost you enormous sums of money.

The book has been divided into two parts.

Part one will deal with the effective ways of finding GREAT service employees. We'll provide examples of procedures that worked in the real world in different parts of the United States.

One thing we learned is that people are the same no matter where they are working.

Part two deals with effective ways to train and keep the GREAT service employees once you have devoted so much time, effort, and dollars into finding them and bringing them on board. Here again the examples and ideas explained are ones we utilized in our own service company. THEY WORK!

In addition, chapter 11 provides you with a sample hiring process manual, much like the one we used in our business. The orientation and actual hiring is CRITICAL to "getting it right" and hopefully this manual will provide you with ideas to create your own professional process.

In the last chapter we provide you with sample job descriptions for various positions that a Building Service Contractor has, needs, or will need as it grows. Again, use them as a guide. I know, I know, its boring stuff until you end up in a court room because you didn't have one as written documentation of the job you were asking an employee to do. The same holds true for the hiring process manual.

I want this book to be a learning experience for you and so I encourage you to make notes, underline, write in the margins, or do whatever works. At the end of each part I have provided my suggestions for applying the ideas in the book to your company. If you have ever attended one of my workshops you know that I am a fanatic when it comes to reviewing what we have learned and discussing how we can apply it in the real world. The whole process of finding, training, and keeping GREAT service employees, thought by many to be a boring process, can be truly exciting and it is my purpose here to show you how it can be. Yes, we have some boring stuff that you have to read and apply but, for the most part, this part of owning and managing a service business is truly an exciting experience.

My entire business career was spent in the Building Service Contracting industry, sometimes and maybe better known as the janitorial service business. If you are in that business or fast food, retail, hospitality, etc., I am confident the processes and procedures outlined in this book will work if you are creative in adapting them to your particular business.

You may strongly disagree with some of the ideas I present and that's okay. The whole purpose here is to get you to thinking about how you can find, train, and keep GREAT employees in YOUR COMPANY. If this book gets you to do that, I will have succeeded. Remember, I said I made lots of mistakes. Take what I give you and MAKE YOUR COMPANY BETTER.

Enjoy the experience, learn well and MAKE IT A GREAT DAY!

PART 1

FINDING GREAT SERVICE EMPOYEES

CHAPTER 1

IT'S A JUNGLE OUT THERE!

At the time of the writing of this book (early 2009), the United States is officially, according to the government, in a recession. Some economists say a depression. That means we will have hundreds of people coming in our doors wanting work, right? Maybe, maybe not. Well, at least they come in wanting a paycheck.

When we talk about finding GREAT service employees who are we really competing against to improve our organization and fill the open positions?

For purposes of this book, when we discuss service employees we are identifying employees that fall in the following types of service industries:

◊   Fast food

◊   Convenience and retail store clerks

◊   Janitorial workers

◊   Hospitality service employees

As I drive around the city I see signs in fast food restaurants saying "help wanted" and the newspaper still runs ads for contract cleaning companies looking for employees.

My point is this…No matter what the unemployment rate is or how many people say they are looking for work, it appears that those of us in service related industries are always in need of GREAT employees.

I have talked with many people that have said that when there is a recession they can get all the people they need. In my opinion, that is all the more reason to have a systematic process of finding GREAT people so that your organization is able to attract the best of all of those GREAT people that are supposedly now available. Remember, it is a jungle out there and whether there are large quantities of GREAT people available or very few, those companies with an organized, systematic method of finding and keeping GREAT employees are the ones that prosper in good times and in bad.

After spending over 40 years in the Building Service Contracting industry performing primarily janitorial and related services and in spending large amounts of time with contractors throughout the country, there is one very basic lesson I have learned---you are not competing against other companies doing your kind of service, you are competing against other companies in the service industry. Let me ask you, if the average college age student comes home saying he or she has been offered a position working in fast food or cleaning toilets, which position do you think their parents are going to suggest they take? Right.

So, if you are a Building Service Contractor you need to have a professional, systematic process of convincing people that you have great careers available. Maybe an advantage you have is steady hours rather than split shifts, etc. Those of you in other service related industries, what advantage do you provide that makes your industry an attractive, long term career?

It is easy to get complacent in an economy when unemployment numbers are running at a high level. We tend to think as employers that we are in the driver's seat but I suggest to you that the economy ALWAYS makes a comeback, sometimes just faster than other times. And when it does, those computer technicians and administrative professionals you hired to do the service work you are in will probably go back to their other careers UNLESS---you have done the things necessary to keep them excited about staying in your industry.

We want to assist you through this book to find the right people and then do the things that will keep as many of them as possible in the future.

Before we jump into some creative ways to find people, it is important that we understand some very important keys in being successful in this process.

"HIRING VS. RECRUITING"

It is common in service industries such as janitorial or food service to look at the positions as ones that will have high turnover thinking "the employee will leave anyway as soon as they find something better so why spend a lot of time in the interview and detailed training program". If that is your attitude, they will leave as soon as they can because they will sense that in the interview.

It is important for us to change the way WE view the positions we have available. I suggest to you that it is time you begin viewing the industry you are in and the positions you have as careers, not jobs. But, you may be saying, I am only hiring part time employees at a low wage and they are just looking for extra money. Let me ask you, how do you think we will ever get people to think of our industry as a career choice if we are not showing them the opportunities that exist? How you treat them now may determine if they want to eventually pursue the industry full time. How a prospective or current employee views their job will often mirror the way YOU view their job. It is important that you begin to RECRUIT employees instead of HIRING employees--- the difference?

THE DEFINITION OF HIRING IS THE ATTEMPT TO FILL VACANCIES BY WHATEVER MEANS POSSIBLE. (REACTIVE)

When you are hiring people you are reacting to the immediate needs of the day. A supervisor comes to you and says, "I need someone to start tonight in the south end location beginning at 6 PM and work till midnight. They will need to know how to dump trash and run a vacuum cleaner". So what do you do?

You begin to go through that stack of applications you have over on the corner of the desk. "Okay, I'll call the first three on the top of the stack. That seems to be a good random way of picking someone. I don't remember them but I kept their application so they must be good".

And of course the first two don't answer but by golly the third one does and you offer the job to them by going through a tough screening process. "Have you ever dumped trash?" you ask. The answer comes back, "Why yes, my wife has me take it to the curb every Thursday morning". "Great, have you ever run a vacuum cleaner?" "I vacuum the carpets every Saturday morning". "Sounds perfect, can you meet your supervisor here at our office at 5:30 this evening?"

At 5:30 they arrive at your office not looking like the best recruit you have ever seen. They sure sounded better over the phone. Reminds me of a movie I saw where the person said upon meeting someone for the first time, "You sounded taller on the phone". You're not sure they are even breathing. You take them over to the mirror you have in the waiting room and ask them to breathe on it. They do but it doesn't fog up. So you breathe on it, see a little fog, and say, "Close enough".

Oh, and you didn't tell them the job was 25 miles from their home and after the second night they realize their 12 miles per gallon older model car is using 4 gallons of gas every night to get to and from work. They let you know what you can do with your job. Or maybe they don't let you know, you just find out when you go check on the work and find no one has been there.

Exaggeration? Maybe, but if you think back I will venture a guess that you have hired someone in a similar manor in the past. Whatever segment of the service industry you are in, I bet you can relate a similar story.

You see, when all you are doing is trying to hire to fill slots, you are getting whomever you can get because all you are ever doing is reacting to the current situation.

Now lets move on to recruiting and how it differs from hiring.

THE DEFINITION OF RECRUITING IS THE SYSTEMATIC PROCESS OF LOCATING, SCREENING, HIRING AND TRAINING POTENTIAL QUALITY, GREAT EMPLOYEES.

You see, hiring is only one step in the recruiting process. Unless you do all the steps mentioned above in a professional, systematic way, you will forever be in a panic, high turnover, never ending cycle of frustration.

I suggest that everyone in your organization should be working toward recruiting and not just hiring. A company that I am very familiar with began the process of recruiting and implementing the processes in this part of the book as well as part 2 and the result of the commitment was reducing their turnover to 25% of the national average for the cleaning industry. It takes a commitment and not a token memo from the front office.

So, in the next chapter let's look at some of the ways we can effectively recruit prospects that can become GREAT employees.

> *Thought for the day:* **When I first got married I would go skinny dipping. Now that I have gained considerable weight, I go chunky dunkin'.**

> -   Dick Ollek

CHAPTER 2
NEWSPAPER ADS

Seeing the title of this chapter you probably said, "I've tried newspaper ads, they are expensive and most of the time don't work". Just humor me a bit while I give you some examples of ads that did work for me and why I think they worked. Let's start with one of my favorites:

---

25 IMMEDIATE OPENINGS

We are recruiting SUPERVISORS & GENERAL CLEANERS. Full time and part time positions available. Career opportunities available to those with a desire to succeed.

Apply at xxxxxxxxxxxxxxxxx anytime between 10 am and 7pm. Also open on Saturday from 9 am to 1 pm. Pre-employment drug screen required.

XXXXXXXXXXXXXXXXXXXXXXXXXXXXXX
XXXXXX

EOE/M-F

Whenever we utilized the newspaper to recruit, this ad or one similar was always used. Why was it successful you ask? I am glad you asked. Here is why I think this type of ad worked.

You will notice we said we had multiple IMMEDIATE openings.

In all my years of recruiting relatively lower wage service employees, I found many of them suffered from low self esteem. Their confidence is shattered. They've been turned down for credit or been told by well meaning relatives and friends that they can't do anything really productive and are stuck where they are. As a result, they never really make an effort in a competitive environment because they "just know" they will fail. But tell them there are multiple openings such as 25 and they believe they can get one out of 25. By listing several openings you will get people to apply that otherwise feel too insecure to walk in your door.

Now for those of you who may be thinking I only have 5 openings, etc. let me relay a true story that happened to me a few years ago.

I was visiting one of my branch offices and in talking with my manager about his accomplishments and disappointments he indicated to me his frustration with the Human Resources manager who just didn't seem to be able to keep up with the needs of the branches growth and normal turnover. He asked if I might have a visit with HR in my usual nice demeanor.

In talking with the Human Resource manager, I found he was relying almost exclusively on one agency to fill the open slots and they were not responding to his needs as fast as he (or my manager) would like. I then asked him to run an ad indicating we have 20 immediate openings. His reply? "But Dick, that would be telling a lie. We only have 13 openings". About that time the Branch Manager came walking by the office and I asked him to step in a moment. My question? "I know you have only 13 openings today but if we ran an ad that said 20 immediate openings, do you have 7 people you would like to replace"? His answer was a quick, "I have 70 people I would like to replace". Now that answer was probably given out of frustration but the point I am making is that even if you run an ad for more openings than you have that day, you will need additional people eventually and part of recruiting is having a backlog of people that you can always call for additional growth and turnover. Frankly, you probably have some current employees you would like to replace right now. Do you?

In the chapter on job fairs I will relay another story that amplifies the importance of putting immediate openings as the heading to your ad.

Another reason the ad worked so well is that we took applications at times of the day that many of our competitors didn't. Look at the ad again and you will see we were open until 7 PM in the evening and on Saturday morning. Now, what difference does that make?

If you are only open from 8 to 5 you are asking a prospective employee to take off from their regular job to come apply for your positions. To do this they will need to take a day off or lie about being sick, etc. in order to do so. If they are unemployed it won't make a difference but let's try to recruit the best GREAT people we can and make it easy for them to apply. By being open until 7 PM you allow them to work their regular job and then apply on their way home. By being open on Saturday even enhances your chances at getting great applicants. We were also open many times on Sunday afternoon by wording the ad something like "out looking for a new home? Trying to figure out how you can make the additional payment for just the house you want? Go to the open house, then come by our office and discuss the part time evening positions we have that will give you the extra money you will need".

Our response to Sunday open house ads was great. We had fewer numbers come in the door but the quality of applicants was such that we could employ nearly all of them.

Not to belabor the point on being open late and on weekends but let me remind you, especially if you are in an industry like janitorial service that performs most of its work at night, that you are asking people to work at night so shouldn't you be available to interview them during the hours you want them to work? It just never made sense to me that we wanted our employees to work from 6 PM to 2 AM but we would only interview them between 8 AM and 5 PM. Strange.

While I am on the subject of hours to interview, another pet peeve is when companies will only interview during certain hours of the day like 9-11 AM or 2-4 PM. You are in need of quality GREAT employees but then make it difficult for them to obtain an interview. Remember, the Human Resource department has as its customer the applicants and employees of the company and the same rules and policies that we employ for other customers should apply here—SATISFY THE CUSTOMER. You don't do that by limiting the time you will talk with them.

Let's look at another ad that worked very effectively:

BUSINESS IS BOOMING

We have excellent opportunities for cleaning technicians and seasoned supervisors on a P/T and F/T schedule.

Hours are flexible, growth is realistic, training is provided, and wages and benefits are very competitive. Discuss a future with a proven leader in the Building Services Industry.

Our interview hours for these positions are 8 AM to 8 PM , Monday-Friday and 9 AM –1 PM on Saturday. Pre-employment drug screen required.

ABC COMPANY
1234 GREAT STREET
NICE TOWN, USA
E0E/M/F

In addition to the key points already mentioned, you will notice the heading of the ad—BUSINESS IS BOOMING. Why head up the ad like this? A couple of reasons:

First, most people like to work for a company that is doing well. There is a greater feeling of security if you know the company is doing well and believe me, in this day and age, with many long time, big name companies failing almost daily, that is a major positive advantage.

Second, it keeps your competitors wondering what you are up to. They begin to wonder if you just secured one of their major customers and they start to ask their staff, "Are we in trouble anywhere? I see ABC company is advertising for people because 'business is booming'".

Now really want to confuse them? Run an ad that says business is booming and we need 20 additional people. It's fun.

Occasionally you will have that position that requires a very special person but with the regulations today you can't say things like, "We want only 18 year olds, or we want only retired people or we want only housewives that know good cleaning".

A friend of mine who owned a janitorial service company in one of the New England states had a unique opening that required a special mature person that could not only clean but could represent the company with a great personality, etc. So he ran this ad:

MARY DOESN'T WORK HERE
ANYMORE

For over 10 years Mary cleaned the prestigious offices of a major corporation in downtown Great City from 6 PM –2 AM, Monday through Friday. Mary not only cleaned the offices but was able to project the professional image our company desires to project. Are you our next Mary? If you think you can follow in Mary's footsteps, please apply between 11 AM – 8 PM, Monday through Friday at

1234 Wonderful Street
Great City, USA

EOE/MF

This ad helped him get only the mature people that it would take for this important position within his company. It did not discriminate in that anyone who felt they could replace Mary in this important position was welcome to apply.

As we conclude this chapter on newspaper ads, lets remember some very important points:

◊ Headlining a number of employees needed brings in those who may suffer from a lack of self-esteem or self confidence who might not otherwise apply.

◊ Interview in hours when applicants can comfortably apply such as after 5 PM and on Saturday mornings or Sunday afternoons.

◊ Market you organization in the ad by letting the community and your applicants know you are an exciting place to work for and that your company is on the move.

Thought for the day: **Maxine on aging, "Take every birthday with a grain of salt. This works much better if the salt is accompanied by a margarita".**

CHAPTER 3

CAREER FAIRS

In this chapter as we discuss career fairs, I will be referring to the process of conducting your own in house career fair as opposed to attending the standard fairs conducted by the local Chamber of Commerce, etc.

I found when we had a booth at the local career or job fair we were competing with all types of companies and most of the time they were companies looking for people with degrees or advanced degrees. Frankly, the service industries generally do not require a college degree, just a strong desire to work and satisfy the customer. Exceptions of course exist, but for the most part we are trying to attract GREAT middle management and entry level employees. I found the best career fair to attract this type of GREAT employee was to conduct my own.

Before we go any further, you may have noticed I call them career fairs and not job fairs. I do this for a very simple reason---I am looking for employees who want to make this THEIR CAREER. Think about it. You probably have some key people in your organization that started with you by applying for a part time position and they grew into a valuable asset. Just look around, I bet you have some. I KNOW I did. So, why not conduct a GREAT employee search with the idea of them becoming long time career employees. It is important to remember that your employees will view their position with your company in the same manner you view their position with the company. If you are just looking for someone to fill a slot, they will sense that and will fill that slot until they find someone who really wants to help them develop into a valuable asset.

I know, I know. We have all been burned by employees who we invested an enormous amount of time and dollars into only to have them leave with no notice, etc. But does that mean we just quit doing it? Do you quit investing in elaborate sales proposals for that account you want because the last 3 you invested a large amount of time and energy into decided to go with someone else? Of course not, so why shouldn't you be pursuing prospective GREAT service employees with the same vigor and enthusiasm?

I always found it curious that a company will invest thousands of dollars into securing a new customer, buy the leather bound proposal books, prepare a PowerPoint sales presentation, bring in the President of the company to "seal the deal" and then cut corners on finding the GREAT employees to service that important customer. Do you do that? Never, right?

I have personally witnessed a situation where a company invested nearly $10,000 in all the "bells and whistles" to secure a very prestigious account only to tell their Human Resources department that they went over budget in the sales department to secure the account, so HR would have to cut their advertising and recruiting dollars to find the people to service the account. Talk about a recipe for disaster. You just told your new customer how wonderful you are with all the right equipment and people and then you shortcut the system on doing the right things to find the right GREAT people.

So…what are the effective steps in conducting your own successful company career fair? I am going to tell you. For purposes of discussion, I am going to assume you are a Building Service Contractor. I might add this is a tremendous way to create team building within you organization. So here we go.

PREPARATION

It is important to have one individual designated the chairperson, someone from Human Resources. If you don't have an HR department, it may be you or someone who can delegate responsibilities and monitor the progress or lack of it. It is important to involve as many of your people as possible. The more people excited about it, the greater the opportunity for success.

I would recommend utilizing a hotel meeting room unless you have room at your place of business to handle sizable numbers of people. Keep in mind, by going to a different location you are sending the message that you are a professional organization on the grow. Also, it makes your competitor wonder what's going on. I love it.

We found Saturdays to be the best from like 10 AM to 4 PM and if you want to expand it you can also add Sunday from noon to 3 PM.

So let's go through what I call the career fair guidelines.

◊ Hold a meeting of all key players to set date(s), times and location to hold the fair. Remember, a central location is usually best or if you are starting a major account, a location close to that account can be helpful.

◊ Select the chairperson to be in charge---then delegate the different tasks such as:

* Calling hotels to get rates on a meeting room, catering, easels, etc. Once rates have been established, visit the hotel of choice to make sure the room is easily accessible and large enough to hold the following:

* Round tables set up in the middle of the room for applicants to sit with pencils and phone books on each one.

* A reception table at the entrance to the room with multi lingual receptionists with applications. A very important point is to make sure that you have applications and

hiring documents in all the languages that you are hoping to attract. Tables in the other 3 corners of the room for immediate private interviewing upon completion of the application.

* Tables to display literature and manuals with a TVCR or other type of electronic media running training videos.

* Table for refreshments and snacks such as popcorn, chips and dip, cookies, etc.

* A wall to display uniforms and set up equipment that the employees will be using in their new career.

◊ Determine the method you will use to advertise the event such as radio, TV, newspaper, and contact them to discuss. We found by putting a notice in the pay envelopes of existing employees and in the company newsletter went a long way toward getting people to attend the event. In fact, we found that current employees would bring friends and relatives to the fair.

◊ Printing a large quantity of applications, post-hire packets, employment policy and procedure packets, etc. and box them all up.

◊ Gather video training tapes, CD's, DVD's and TVCR's.

◊ Meet at least weekly to get updates on assigned tasks.

The week of the fair gather all material, supplies, equipment, etc. in a central location. Check off items to assure everything needed is there.

☐ **Applications**
☐ **Post-Hire packets**

☐ **Paper clips**
☐ **Stapler & extra staples**

☐ **Employment policy & procedure handbooks**

☐ **Laptop computer for badges**

☐ **Listing of positions available**

☐ **Business cards of managers, supervisors, etc.**

☐ **Pencils & sharpeners**   ☐ **TVCR's**
☐ **Phone books**   ☐ **Video tapes (multi-lingual)**

☐ **Copy machine for ID's**   ☐ **Literature & manuals**
☐ **Digital camera & disks**   ☐ **Equipment for display**

☐ **Uniforms for display & for**   ☐ **Chemicals for display**
   new employees   ☐ **Badge holders & clips**

☐ **Laminating machine**   ☐ **Extra extension cords for**
                                                      TVCR's, equipment, etc.

◊   Load everything the night before or early the morning of the career fair and be at the hotel at least 2 hours before opening.

◊   Set everything up in the room and test all TVCR's, etc. to assure they work properly.

◊   Check with catering to assure refreshments and food items will be checked often and kept stocked.

◊   Have a brief staff meeting to discuss items such as overflow of applicants and getting them interviewed without having to wait for hours. Also, who monitors the videos, etc.?

I indicated in Chapter 2 that I would have a story to tell about the immediate opening heading I frequently used in our ads so here goes:

Several years ago my company secured a large contract in Las Vegas, Nevada that would require about 75 people to begin as soon as we were able to bring them on board. This was coupled with the fact the other part of the contract had us needing 150 people at their facility in Phoenix, Arizona.

As we were planning the career fairs we were going to conduct in each city, we were told by our customer as well as numerous other "experts" that Las Vegas would be nearly impossible to obtain labor for the contract. With us paying about $4 per hour under the normal union scale that the casino hotels were paying we would politely, and not so politely, be told "good luck in finding the people you need". So…now what?

We decided to run the following ad:

---

75 IMMEDIATE OPENINGS
FOR CLEANERS AT
XXXXXXXXXXXXXXXXX

WE NEED:

Cleaners	Supervisors
Team Leaders	Support Staff

WE OFFER:

Above Average Wages	Paid Vacations
Attendance Bonuses	New Uniforms
Medical Insurance	Flexible Hours
Paid Holidays	New Equipment

We are anxious to visit with you if you are dependable, eager to learn, and want to get ahead. Come visit us on

Sunday, August 25 from 1 p.m. – 5 p.m.
Monday, August 26 from 10 a.m. – 7 p.m.
At the
xxxxxxxxxxxxxxxxxxxxxxxxxxxx
123 Anywhere Road
Las Vegas, NV 89109
xxxxxxxxxxxxx Meeting Room
(Enter on south side of the building, then follow the xxxxx signs)
EOE/MF

In addition we decided to put the bulk of our people in Phoenix where we would have the biggest draw and needed the most people. We would send my administrative assistant (my daughter) and me to Las Vegas to interview the few people we would have come to apply. The staff also figured I was probably the least competent of our group and with

Robyn, my assistant, there, how much trouble could I cause anyway or how badly could I mess it up. I readily accepted my assignment to Vegas. If nothing else, the hotel we were using had a nice array of video poker machines.

You will notice from the ad that we were interviewing beginning on Sunday afternoon. That morning we decided to have a late breakfast/ early lunch, but prior to that we thought we would go by the hotel to assure that everything was in place for the event. We had taken the only meeting room available at the hotel for those dates which was at the back of the property so we had signs made and spaced throughout the property directing people to the right place.

As we approached we noticed a long line of people winding from the front toward the back of the hotel. We commented that they must have quite an event taking place which probably explains why we were unable to secure a meeting room at the front of the hotel. As we got closer to our room, people started asking us if we were the people that were going to be interviewing for the 75 immediate openings. We soon realized the long line was waiting for US and it was still nearly 3 hours before we were to begin interviewing. So much for breakfast/lunch. Those of you that know me personally are certainly aware of the fact that I do love to eat. Bummer.

You can probably imagine the scrambling that took place over the next several minutes. We opened for business and began interviewing. We needed to improvise a great deal those two days and actually had to stay over a couple of extra days to complete all the interviews, but…we hired 75 plus people.

Those two days provided us with nearly 700 applicants and when we asked them why they applied here, the overwhelming response was that our ad said "Immediate Openings" and they needed work NOW. We found out also that even though the similar jobs at the casino hotels paid considerably more, there was also about a 2-3 year wait for a position because current employees would recommend their family and friends and those people were hired before the regular applicants. Oh sure, we might lose them to better paying positions in the future but we had them for 2 or 3 years and in the meantime had the opportunity to show them the advantages of a career with us.

As we were interviewing the applicants, I would sometimes ask, "How long have you lived in Las Vegas?", and when they looked at their watch I knew they were not long time residents. In fact, several told me as they looked at their watch that they had just got off the plane that morning and were relocating to Las Vegas. I didn't hire many of those applicants. Even I couldn't fog up the mirror for them.

Oh by the way, they had only about 200 people apply in Phoenix and it turned out to be tougher to complete the roster there than in Las Vegas.

There are some really important things to remember as you consider doing a career fair for your company:

◊ Get as many of your staff involved as possible. It is a great opportunity for bonding.

◊ Always plan ahead thoroughly so you are sending the message that you are an organized company.

◊ Don't allow language to be a barrier. Have applications AND staff members at the fair that speak all the languages fluently of the people you are attempting to reach.

◊ MAKE IT FUN

I always enjoyed the career fairs we conducted. Not only did we recruit new, qualified GREAT people to our staff, it provided a time for me to learn more about the people we already had on our staff.

Thought for the day: **Sign in a Florida dry cleaning establishment--**

Answers----75 cents
Answers requiring thought---$1.25
Correct answers---$2.15
Dumb looks---free

- Author Unknown

CHAPTER 4
RECRUITING NEIGHBORHOODS

There are several effective ways to recruit specific neighborhoods or certain areas of town. This can really be important if you have some new business in a certain area of town and want to employ GREAT people right from that neighborhood. It attracts the residents because it allows them to secure a full or part time position close to home. In this day of rapidly fluctuating gas prices, that can have a tremendous effect on turnover. So let's review some different methods of recruiting neighborhoods and finding those GREAT people.

"DOOR HANGARS"

An effective tool is to print up door hangars with information containing the hours you are recruiting for i.e. 6-10 PM Monday through Friday, etc. along with a general area of where the job is located. You can then put the location to apply and when to apply. Remember, if you are recruiting for 6-10 PM it is imperative you have someone available to interview and hire during those hours.

You can use wording on the hangar like, "Tired of watching reruns of CSI or Law and Order? Apply now to earn additional income in a position that can lead to a GREAT new career". Be creative with something that grabs their attention.

I suggest then that the hangars be placed on their door knobs during the daylight hours so they are there when they arrive home from their daytime job. Who knows, you might even find someone home during the day that could be available for that daytime position for which you haven't been able to find a suitable person.

Be sure the people that distribute the door knob hangars know something about your company. My experience has shown that you will, in fact, encounter individuals that want to know something about who you are and what you do. I never let the people distributing discuss pay. Their instructions should be that, "We are glad you are showing an interest in our company and we would like you to follow the detailed instructions on the door hangar. We don't want to give you any incorrect information".

"PENNY POWER/PENNY SAVER"

Another way to recruit neighborhoods is to place ads in the Penny Power or Penny Saver and other neighborhood thrift magazines that are so popular for people to sell and buy appliances, tires, etc. You can purchase specific neighborhoods to keep the cost contained and effective. This again is an important tool for recruiting given the uncertainty of transportation costs in today's environment.

"NEIGHBORHOOD STRIP MALLS"

Nearly every neighborhood in every community has a small strip mall that has a vacant storefront or two. As the new larger malls have been developed, many of these smaller malls, once the pride of the community, have fallen on hard times. But the fact remains that many people still continue to live in those neighborhoods and are excellent potential GREAT employees.

I remember doing a workshop on this subject and one of the people in the audience was unfamiliar with the term "strip mall" and thought I was referring to a different kind of strip business establishment. She was quite vocal in her criticism of me until several of the workshop participants were able to explain in detail what a strip mall really is. Until then I had never really thought of the other strip business as a potential source of employees. Still don't.

If you are in a city where you need employees where the applicants must travel some distance to your main office to complete an application let me suggest you explore one of these vacant units. Again, we must go to where our labor supply is located. What may be a reasonable distance for you to travel may be considered a long distance for someone with poor transportation or minimal gas money. GO TO THEM.

Contact the leasing agent for the mall and tell them you want a month to month lease on one of their vacant units and that you will only be using it 2 days a week and if they lease your space you will gladly move to another of their vacant units. Some rent for them is better than no rent.

Then put a sign in the window indicating you are interviewing every Tuesday and Thursday from 2-7 PM, etc., etc. Have a desk, several tables, applications, and all the other items needed to screen and hire new members of your team. IT WORKS.

"ETHNIC RADIO STATIONS'

This is a very effective tool for recruiting GREAT service employees. Many cities now have stations that cater to particular ethnic groups and those stations have a loyal following. We were very effective in the southwest United States in recruiting hispanic team members, many of whom became supervisors and middle management leaders in our company.

In some cases the stations consider announcements that offer their listeners employment a public service announcement and therefore offer it free. I am seeing a trend away from that policy but it never hurts to ask.

If you are going to utilize this method of building your GREAT employee base let me suggest two things:

◊ Do not include a phone number in your radio spot but rather give an address where they can apply. Remember I said in the introduction that I made a lot of mistakes. This was one of them. We used the phone number the first time and overloaded the system. I would rather overload my application room than the phone system.

◊ Be sure that the person(s) greeting the applicants is fluent in the language of the ethnic group you are trying to reach. I have had Building Service Contractors tell me that trying to reach out to ethnic communities just didn't work for them. In visiting further with them I usually found they didn't have anyone who could speak the language nor did they have the applications and training materials in that language. (More on this later).

In closing out this section on ethnic radio station recruiting, let me tell you that the last 17 years that I owned my own Building Service Contracting company I personally headquartered out of our Phoenix, Arizona office where I had a 99% non English speaking work force (the 1% was me and a few other people) and we managed exceptionally well. In fact, some of the best Christmas gatherings and summer picnics I attended were in this branch. Somehow I find when you want to communicate with other people, the language barrier can be overcome.

"BE A HEADHUNTER"

As a leader in your company you should always be actively pursuing GREAT service employees when you are out in the community. Call your friends and ask if they know of anyone that is looking for an opportunity for a career, be alert to anyone you meet at the grocery store, restaurant or other service establishment that is exhibiting great service. Don't be afraid to ask them to interview with your organization.

One technique that I found that works effectively is to print business cards that on the front say, "THANKS FOR GREAT SERVICE". Then in smaller letters say something like, "My company is looking for GREAT career minded people that display the positive attitude you have shown to me. If you are interested in a new exciting career, please contact me at the address shown on the reverse side of this card". IT WORKS.

I recall standing in line at a restaurant one day with a client while waiting for a table for lunch. Our discussion turned to different, effective ways to recruit GREAT middle managers. During that conversation I mentioned to him that several of my very best managers had come from the restaurant business because they understood labor costs, managing people and customer satisfaction.

After lunch, and as we were about to walk out the door, the assistant manager of the restaurant stopped me and told me he had overheard my conversation earlier and wanted to know if I would consider visiting with him about any middle management positions I might have available. What do you think my answer was? I gave him one of my cards and asked him to contact me at his earliest convenience and we would visit. He did and became a valuable member of our team.

Not long ago I mentioned this at one of my recruiting workshops and I had an attendee say to me, "Isn't that a bit unethical to walk into a restaurant and recruit their good employees"? My response was, "It is my considered opinion that if the shoe was on the other foot, the restaurant manager would have no hesitation in trying to recruit one of my GREAT people". We live in a world of finding the best people for our organization. That means using different tools and techniques in the ongoing recruiting process.

"FLEA MARKETS"

Many local neighborhoods have weekend flea markets that allow you to rent a booth for a minimal amount. Many of the GREAT line workers you are looking for will be frequenting these markets and it is an outstanding way to reach a large potential employee base for a minimal investment---and usually you won't catch any fleas, just GREAT people. If you haven't tried this method of recruiting I encourage you to put it on your "to do" list.

"THE OVER 55 GROUP"

Before we leave this discussion on neighborhood recruiting I want to say a few words about the over 55 group. That's my age group and we're a hearty lot and there are an increasing number of us available each year for you to utilize.

As an example, have you noticed when you visit a fast food restaurant how the work force is sprinkled with this well seasoned generation? It isn't because they are trying to sell old hamburgers or hamburgers to older people. It's because they have found them to be reliable, dependable major contributors to the success of their operation.

As we see more and more fast food establishments opening for a 5 or 6 AM breakfast menu, we find more and more 55 plus workers staffing the store. I venture to guess it may be hard to get the younger generation to arrive for work by 4:30 or 5 AM in the morning. Just a guess, but I raised 3 children. 'Nuff said?

At the risk of sounding partial or prejudicial, the older generation grew up dedicated to getting up earlier, getting to work, doing what was expected of them and not leaving until the job was done. It came first. It may be one of the faults of that generation but I happen to agree with their work ethic.

Several years ago, after my father had retired from his job, and had about fished out the lakes around where he lived, he asked if I had anything he could do for about 6 hours a day. He missed the daily routine, and knowing my Dad, he missed being around people.

As luck would have it, I had a day porter position that was 6 hours per day and 4 hours on Saturday. It was also about 15 miles out of town at a large industrial facility. We had been having difficulty keeping someone in that position so Dad came along at exactly the right time.

Dad worked that position for about 3 years, never missed a day and stayed when needed to do whatever needed to be done for the customer. He was around people all day which he thoroughly enjoyed and frankly, was my eyes and ears at what, was at that time, one of my largest customers.

When Dad decided to retire for good and spend the winters with Mom in Texas, I notified my customer that he was retiring for good this time and that we would work diligently to find a replacement just as good. My customer's response? "You won't find anyone like him. He understands what it takes to do the job, to satisfy the customer, he never complains, goes out of his way to do whatever we want within the scope of work. He comes from a generation that is no more".

Were they right about the generational differences? Probably, but having said all that, this new generation is extremely bright and capable if we recruit and train them correctly.

By the way, I did find a great replacement. A gentlemen, 70 years old who liked to complain about everything with a smile on his face and then go and willingly do the work. Could have done without some of the complaining, but he did a great job for many years before he too wanted to retire to Texas.

> *Thought for the day*: **Ever buy a bird dog at a pet store, take it home only to find out it won't fly?**

- Dick Ollek

CHAPTER 5

ON LINE RECRUITING

The fact that I have placed this recruiting technique near the end of this part of the book does not mean that I consider it last in the way to find GREAT service employees. This method can be a very effective tool in securing GREAT middle management staff.

I say middle management staff because I still do not believe that the average line worker uses a computer to complete an application for employment. I do believe that it is coming but I don't believe we are there yet. However, having said that, many larger companies now have computers in their lobbies or near the front door where you complete an application on line and then are called for an interview at a later time. This is a process that will spread to most companies in the future as we continue to become a society that communicates via electronics. If I can be allowed to editorialize a bit, I think it will be interesting in the future to see how we all get along with each other since we are no longer developing true interpersonal communication skills. Seems we don't talk to each other anymore. I often wonder why people e-mail each other when they sit right next to each other. Wouldn't it be easier just to talk? Remember, I said I'm from the old generation.

Now having said that, I am a firm believer that your application should be on your web page in a prominent spot AND in all the languages you utilize in your organization. For those line workers who do want to apply on the web you will be ready.

In addition, I believe you should mention in your print ads, door hangars, radio ads, business cards, and any other media form you use, that applications can be completed and submitted on line. I suggest you update your web site weekly with career openings available. Encourage your employees to have their friends and relatives check the web site for updates.

Some companies now are placing ongoing small ads in the newspaper and Penny Power/Penny Saver, etc. for the express purpose of asking people to go to their web site to see all the great current opportunities available with their great company.

With an on going contract with the paper you can secure a lower rate and it gets people to your web site to submit the application. Never know, it might even get a prospective customer to go to your web site to see what you are all about. There is no question in my mind that this method of securing applications is going to grow in spite of us old traditionalists.

I was able to secure sales people and middle management people by advertising with sites such as Monster.com, etc. I found the investment minimal compared to other forms of media and also learned that this group of candidates is far more inclined to search the internet. In fact, this is, for many of them the only way they look for employment. We found we had to sift through an enormous number of applications to find a few qualified applicants but, believe me, I would rather do that any day than to have openings and no one to talk with.

STAY TUNED

Thought for the day: **Maxine on Housework—I do my housework in the nude. It gives me incentive to clean the mirrors as quickly as possible.**

CHAPTER 6
MANAGING THE RECRUITING PROCESS

If you begin to use the techniques discussed in the previous chapters you will start to get an influx of potential GREAT employees. How to manage this group is just as important as how you got them in the first place. I suggest you establish a system that allows you to track the people who have applied and their qualifications. This will help you to match them up with appropriate positions quickly and easily.

While ACT software was really designed for tracking sales prospects and their activity, I found it a tremendously effective way of managing and tracking employee applicants. By entering all of your applicants in this database you can then sort them by:

- ◆ Position desired or position qualified to hold

- ◆ Zip code or geographic region where they reside

- ◆ Telephone number

♦ Desired shift

♦ Full time or part time work desired

Think of the convenience. If a supervisor or manager requests a part time vacuum specialist from 6-10 PM, Monday through Friday, in a certain area of town, you can go to the database and select part time, geographic region, position, shift, and you have all of the applicants available at the current time.

You can go on the internet and do a search for ACT and get the details on their latest edition. At the time of this writing I believe they were on version 11.0.

I should mention there are other software programs on the market and I mention ACT only because that is the one I used and am familiar with. Remember, I said in the introduction that what you would get here is what worked for me and not necessarily the only system that works.

As I mentioned earlier, here is the process being used by many companies in the cleaning industry today. A request comes in for a part time vacuum specialist for a certain account needed immediately. We go to the corner of our desk where we have placed the most recent pile of applicants and grab the top one. They want full time work and live 30 miles from the work location but we are determined to fill that position so the supervisor will have somebody TONIGHT.

We call the applicant who readily accepts the position and we tell the supervisor that we have a wonderful experienced new team member that can start TONIGHT. After 2 nights (if they show up the second night) they realize that it takes 5 gallons of gas to make the round trip to and from work every night for the 4 hour position and they then tell you what you can do with your job.

Wouldn't it have been much simpler to have gone to a database and sorted the qualified applicants and then hired one that fit the qualifications AND lived close to the work location? Don't you think your chances of retaining that GREAT employee are much greater using a system for screening potential applicants?

"KEEPING IN CONTACT"

Once you have accumulated a supply of applicants and have entered them into a database, I suggest you begin a process of keeping in contact with them on a regular basis for, let's say, six months after the original application date. How should we do that you ask? I am glad you asked.

Start by sending them a "thank you" letter for applying. Indicate in the letter the length of time you retain applications and they are welcome to contact you at any time to check on the status of their application.

Then put them on the mailing list for your company newsletter. Don't have a newsletter? Start one. Even if it is only a one page "notes and news" type of bulletin it lets your current employees, customers, designated customer prospects and employee prospects know what is going on in the organization. I assure you it will pay dividends.

A prospective employee will WANT to work for you if they are getting regular correspondence from you. Current GREAT employees can pass the newsletter on to friends and relatives and invite them to apply. Now and then a prospective customer will even call and invite you to present a proposal for service. I had that happen on several occasions and secured some very nice business through my monthly newsletter.

I think it is important to remember in the service business where we rely on labor rather than a product to produce our revenue, it is critical that we market and sell to prospective and current employees just as we would to prospective and current customers.

It is my thinking that this chapter on managing the recruiting process will meet with opposition as you contemplate implementing the ideas in this book. I say that because as I travel the country working with various Building Service Contractors, many still use the corner of the desk stack of applications process no matter what size their organization is. Some have very professional, sophisticated systems and processes for managing unemployment claims, health care benefits, and payroll systems but have difficulty in systematizing the recruiting process. If you are one of those contractors, humor me, try a software tracking system----and USE IT.

Thought for the day: **I have a theory that has borne itself out pretty much over the years. If a prospective customer tells me that price is not the issue…it is.**

- Ollekism

CHAPTER 7

AND YOUR FACILITES LOOK LIKE?

In the previous chapters we discussed the importance of an ongoing marketing and sales program for prospective and current GREAT employees, as well as a systematic method of tracking the applicants. Another very important part of the selling process is the facility where you interview and process new employees, especially if you are in the cleaning business.

Stop reading for a moment and take a walk to the front of the building where you ask prospective GREAT team members to apply for a position with your company. When they drive up, what do they see? Nicely painted building, accurate well positioned signage, well lighted grounds, neatly mowed and maintained? Please make a note of any improvements that need to be made and who will make them promptly.

Next, walk in the door that applicants enter to complete their applications. Okay, so we have a few cobwebs hanging from the ceiling and we haven't had time to vacuum the carpet this week but we've been busy starting that new large account. I understand completely but I want to remind you that if you are in the cleaning business and your business is to keep things clean, isn't it important that we begin at our own office so our prospective GREAT team members get the message loud and clear that we provide first class, quality, professional service and satisfaction to our customers and expect nothing less from anyone joining our team? If you are in the fast food business, your kitchen is judged by the appearance of the eating areas and your restroom facilities. I am not suggesting new facilities. What I am suggesting is that the facilities you have should be clean, orderly and inviting.

This reminds me of one of my long time customers who also became a long time friend. Part of the customer satisfaction process was for me to do a monthly inspection tour with him which, if things went well, culminated with a lunch (I bought).

I should mention that this was a large industrial facility sprawled out over several acres and we cleaned the administrative areas, factory offices, lunchrooms, restrooms, etc. with a sizable staff around the clock.

When I would arrive for the monthly tour, my customer's first order of business was to walk to the main supply closet in the factory and check its condition. If everything looked neat and clean, mop buckets and trash barrels empty, etc. he would say, "Ollek, looks to me like your crews are doing a great job, let's go to lunch". By the way, my part of the deal was that I could not alert my crew as to the day I was coming. I kept my word on that issue although I sometimes I wish I hadn't.

On the other hand, if he found anything out of order such as our equipment dirty or mop buckets standing full of water with a mop in them, we would spend the rest of the day walking the entire facility. You see, his philosophy was that if we couldn't keep a 20 x 20 supply closet clean, how in the world could we keep his large plant facility clean. Agree? He taught me quickly the importance of a clean janitor's closet and it became one of my missions throughout my career. It was generally the first place I looked when I visited one of our accounts.

You see, it does hold true. If we can't keep our own facilities clean and inviting, how in the world can we expect our GREAT team members to keep our customer's facilities clean? WE set the example in our office as to what we expect in the field.

It is also critical that the person greeting new prospective GREAT employees should great them with a smile, thank them for coming in, and give them clear instructions on the process of completing the application and the ensuing interview. There should be no question that they are welcome.

Let me share some of my ideas as to how the application area should look in addition to being clean, etc.

First, I suggest you have a TVCR or other means of video playing continuously that talks about your company. If you don't have a full blown orientation video or sales video, a short welcome video done in house will do just fine running on a loop all day. Let me suggest if you have some training videos that you use such as one on backpack vacuuming or scrubbing and recoating of tile floors, have it run as well. Not trying to make experts out them while completing their application, but we want them to be fully aware of the business we are in.

We actually had large placards made with the outline of our line worker training program on them so as to give the prospective GREAT employee an idea of what they could expect if they joined our team. And yes, we had it in different languages to reflect the different nationalities we had on our team. Made for full walls in some of the branches.

These coupled with the videos running showing our orientation of team members gave the applicant a very thorough overview of what he or she could expect to be doing if they joined our organization. Yes, some walked out of the applicant room but I would rather have them walk out of there than a customer's place of business.

One thing I observed years ago, whether in the cleaning business or in the fast food business, many times the children come along with the applicant. If this is the case, why not put a popcorn machine in the waiting area along with a water cooler? Oh, and make popcorn for them. Messy, but they'll never forget the experience. If you are in fast food, offer the children a small drink, etc. Remember, you are recruiting and recruiting is an ongoing process and you never know if the children might some day also become GREAT employees.

One great example of this are the grocery stores that provide mini carts for children to go along side their parents while shopping. I venture to say, it isn't to sell them a cart or that they have an excess of plastic, but rather to get them in the habit of shopping at their store so when they begin their adult life, etc. they just continue the shopping process at that food store. Great idea. That's long range planning at its best.

A few years ago I conducted a workshop on recruiting and discussed at length the ideas we are talking about in this chapter including the effective use of a popcorn machine and soda or water fountain for the children. A year or so later I was at a meeting where a gentleman informed me that one of his key people had attended my workshop and that as a result he remodeled his applicant room so he would have room for a soda and popcorn machine. They were using both and that while it was designed to make the applicants more comfortable, he had noticed a dramatic improvement in the attitude of his staff doing the reception and interviewing duties. A side benefit that I really had not anticipated but it makes sense. No...I don't sell popcorn machines, just looking for better and more effective ways to find and retain GREAT employees.

I don't want to belabor the point but I cannot over emphasize the importance of presenting a clean, neat, and appealing first impression for people who enter your premises. Never know, a prospective or current customer just might decide to pay you a personal visit. How do your facilities stack up?

Thought for the day: **"The older I get the better I was."**

-     - Joe Garigiola

CHAPTER 8
TIME FOR THE INTERVIEW

Up to this point you have spent an enormous amount of energy, time, and dollars to utilize various procedures for bringing GREAT people in your door for an interview. If I have been effective in presenting my recommendations, you have even improved the appearance of your facility. Now is the time when you have the opportunity to "sell" the benefits of someone beginning a career with your organization. Don't blow it.

The people who walk in your door to complete an application are your CUSTOMERS and should be treated with the utmost respect. If they don't return the favor, you just won't be employing them but don't prejudge them before the interview begins.

It is also important to remember that different nationalities may have different customs when they apply for work. For instance, in the United States we have long been told that if someone won't look you in the eye when you are talking to them or they to you, you probably can't trust them. In some countries the people are taught that out of respect when applying for work never look the interviewer in the eye. To do so, would show a great deal of disrespect and would hinder severely the chances for obtaining employment.

If you are a company that is actively recruiting different cultures, I urge you to do some homework on the customs they have grown up learning.

I have had the privilege to work with many different companies and observe the way they do the interview process. It has been very interesting for me to observe the good, the bad and the ugly.

Not long ago I sat in on an interview where a branch manager was interviewing someone he was hoping would join his management team. His interview went something like this,

"How long have you been married? Will your wife object to the evening hours? How old are your kids? Won't they miss daddy? I heard a rumor you were arrested for drunk and disorderly, is that all behind you now"? You get the picture. It is the worst interview I have ever sat through. The prospect chose not to accept the position, the owner of the company I was working for took the manager who did the interview to lunch and bought his to go. Harsh treatment? To the best of my knowledge, this individual had been given training on the correct interview process on several occasions.

At the risk of being too elementary, I will include in this chapter some of what I consider do's and don'ts in an interview. I will also include some of what I consider the Equal Employment Opportunity Commission's (EEOC) guidelines for interviewing. Let me caution you as we discuss these guidelines that rules, regulations and employment laws change as time passes and different political administrations are in control in Washington D.C. I emphasize my disclaimer as outlined in the front of the book. The suggestions I make are as I understand them and may or may not be in place at the time you read this book.

Since I mentioned Washington D.C. above I must tell of the time that I was watching the Tonight Show with Jay Leno. During one of his jaywalking segments that he frequently does, he was asking various college students what the D.C. stood for behind Washington. Many students did not know but the one that really struck me was the young lady who took a guess that it stood for, "Da Capitol"? She was dead serious. Da capitol is in Washington but she did not have the correct answer. Just had to throw that in.

I realize the government changes the rules but here are some of the questions I learned I should not or could not ask:

- ◆ Age or date of birth

- ◆ Birthplace

- ◆ Religion or race

- ◆ Marital status or maiden name

- ◆ Number or ages of children

- ◆ If they have child care arranged

- ◆ Spouse's name or place of employment

- ◆ Parents' residence

- ◆ Loans, financial obligations, wage attachments, or personal bankruptcies

- ◆ If they speak a foreign language unless it is relevant to the job

- ◆ Mother's surname

- ◆ Membership in social organizations

- ◆ Psychological well-being

- ◆ Past injuries or diseases

- ◆ Prior workers' compensation claims

- ◆ Health status such as how many days out for sick leave last year

- ◆ Visible physical characteristics such as scars, burns, etc.

- ◆ If the person is a citizen, however you can ask if he or she is legal to work in the United States

My policy and the policy I asked my staff to follow was that if you feel a question borders on one that should not be asked---DON'T ASK IT. The reality of today's society is that many people like to file lawsuits and it is best to play it safe.

Now, how do you get answers to the questions we have listed as not to ask? I generally used more of a conversational style of interview, which more often than not, resulted in having the information volunteered without asking. Seldom did I leave an interview with a prospective GREAT employee without having the information that I wanted and it included most of the information outlined above and I didn't have to ask one borderline question.

Now what are some of those questions we asked that got answers without having to ask a nonaskable question (nonaskable is a new word you heard here first).

1) **Why are you considering leaving your present position (If they are currently working)?**

2) **Tell me in detail what you did/do at your last (current) position?**

3) **What did you like to do best?**

4) **What did you like to do least?**

5) **What do you consider to be your greatest accomplishment in your life to this point?**

6) **What do you consider to be your greatest disappointment in your life to this point?**

7) **What type of person is hardest for you to deal with?**

8) **Tell me about the boss you liked best.**

9) **What sort of work would your family like to see you doing?**

There are other pointed questions but I found many of the answers I was looking for usually came as a result of these few questions. I didn't fire the questions at them but rather asked one and then "had a conversation" with them about it. In that way it didn't appear to be an interview but rather a friendly conversation.

At the end of this chapter I have included an INFORMAL APPLICANT SURVEY that we asked our prospective GREAT team members to complete. You will note they were under no obligation to complete it but nearly all did. This survey, along with a completed application and answers to the questions I've listed above gave me a pretty thorough insight into the applicant and whether they would make a GREAT member of our team.

Now your question is, "How can you take that much time with each applicant"? I am only hiring a line worker to clean a building four, six, or eight hours per night, etc."? Exactly, and my response is that one of the reasons we are constantly having to look for GREAT team members over and over is that we don't take the time to do the job right up front. Once you get the system down you can go through this process very rapidly and the reality of the matter is that many applicants won't measure up by the time you get through 2 or 3 of the questions and the interview is terminated.

"THE COST OF TURNOVER"

Another major reason it is so important to take the time to do it right the first time is the dollars associated with turnover. We will explain in greater detail in Part 2 of this book this reality but it is important to mention it here when we are discussing the initial interview.

Throughout the years, studies have shown that in the Building Service Contracting industry, the cost of recruiting, interviewing, and providing the initial orientation and training for one employee is approximately $500. I had used that number for several years in the workshops I do and was curious recently if that number still was reasonably accurate.

So, I asked two of my esteemed, trusted colleagues in the industry to provide me with what they thought was the correct number. I gave them no hints as to what I was thinking and did not tell them I was asking the other person to provide a number as well. One person told me $510 and the other said $503. So based on those validations I will stick with the number of $500.

So, let me ask you…how many W-2's did your company make last year? If you employ 100 people and you made 300 W-2s, you had a turnover of 200% and the cost to you for turnover last year was $100,000 plus possible lost customers because of high turnover. I am suggesting that you would have liked to have added that number to your profit picture. Right?

At some of my workshops, participants will challenge the $500 number, so I always ask them to put their number to it--$100, $200, $250. The next thing I ask them to do is multiply their number times the number of W-2's they produced that exceeded their normal work force number. Almost always it is a BFN (Big freakin' number). 'Nuff said.

This entire process of the interview is so critical to a company's success yet is treated in such a haphazard way in so many organizations. I sincerely hope that your company is one that understands the importance of the process and is constantly working to improve. Believe me, it will determine the success, or failure, of your company.

I know when I said it will determine the success or failure of your company, I have some people reading this who will argue that point but let me ask you a question. Ever had a customer terminate your service and tell you something like, "I know you want to do this job for us but your turnover of help is just terrible. It seems like every week there is someone new in my facility".

Or worse yet, they terminate your service and don't tell you why. Bad service maybe? If so, could that be because of a high turnover of untrained employees? Well? We'll talk more about that in Part 2.

INFORMAL APPLICANT SURVEY

Last Name: _____ First Name _____

The following is strictly for information purposes only. You are under no obligation to answer any of the following questions.

1. Have you applied for a position with our company in the past?

2. Are you working now?

3. When could you begin work at our company?

4. What type of relationship do you have with your supervisor in your present (or last) position?

5. Have you ever been fired?

6. If so why?

7. Would your previous employers rehire you if you applied and a position was open?

8. How many days have you been absent from work for any reason in the past year?

9. How many times have you been late for work for any reason in the past year?

10. How will your supervisor rate your performance on your present (or last) job?

11. Have you ever supervised the work of others?

12. Do you consider yourself the best at what you do at work?

13. Do you prefer to work as a team or alone?

14. What are you looking for in a job?

15. Is the location of your assigned building important to you?

16. Are you willing to commute across town to work at a location?

17. If not, how far are you willing to travel?

Thought for the day: Never share your problems with other people. Half of the people don't care and the other half are glad you have them.

- Source Unknown

CHAPTER 9
A PLAN OF ACTION

If you have attended one of my workshops, you know that I am constantly asking attendees to write a review of each of the sections we discuss. Well…this is no different. I am asking you now to list below the important points in the first part of this book:

1. **What are some new and different ways that I am going to change and improve the way I recruit prospective GREAT team members to my company?**

2. **Who will I need to have assist me in making these changes?**

3. What are the obstacles we will need to overcome?

4. How will we overcome those obstacles?

5. When will we have the changes implemented?

6. What changes do I need to make to the appearance of the outside and inside of my facilities to make them more inviting to prospective GREAT team members?

7. Who will I need to assist me in making these changes?

8. When will I have the changes made?

9. **What changes do I need to make in the way my staff greets prospective GREAT team members?**

10. **What changes do I need to make in the interview process to send a positive message to potential GREAT team members?**

11. **What training and other assistance will we need?**

12. **Who can provide that assistance?**

13. **When will we have the changes made?**

Let me suggest you buy a postcard, address it to yourself, then briefly list on the left hand side of the card your answers to the questions listed above. Give the postcard to a friend and ask them to mail it to you in 30 days. When you get the post card, you can judge how you have been doing and what still needs to be accomplished.

Thought for the day: **If you find a path with no obstacles, it probably doesn't lead anywhere!**

- Frank A. Clark

PART 2

THE ORIENTATION, TRAINING AND KEEPING PROCESS

CHAPTER 10
THE FIRST STEP

As I travel the country working with different companies and doing workshops on finding and keeping GREAT employees, one of the first questions I am almost always asked is, "We have such high turnover, what are the most effective ways to keep our people from leaving"? That is certainly an excellent question and there are many companies being very creative in "dangling the carrot" so to speak but it is my firm belief that before we can determine what it takes to keep our GREAT employees, it is important to first find out WHY DO THEY LEAVE IN THE FIRST PLACE?

In my workshops one of the key group exercises we do is breaking up into teams and then having each team list the reasons they believe employees quit. They are then asked to appoint a spokesperson and present to all participants their top two reasons for people leaving.

Let me ask you to do the same exercise right now. What do you think the top reasons are---pay, transportation problems, got a better job, the work is too hard? I suggest you gather your staff together and do the exercise. Amazing the answers you will get. Maybe it's amazing the answers you gave.

ALMOST ALWAYS the number one reason given by the various groups, no matter what part of the country I am in, is PAY. Was that yours?

After an entire adult life spent in the service business, speaking and working with literally hundreds of individuals and their companies, reading and conducting a multitude of surveys, I have found what I believe are the top reasons people leave our employment. Let me share them with you.

"NOBODY TOLD ME WHAT TO DO"

This is not to be confused with "nobody trained me on what to do". This goes deeper to the root of the problem. This says that when the employee was hired, they were told something like, "Go to ABC building and do janitorial work, you'll find everything you need in the closet". That's about the same as in an interview asking an applicant about their experience and having them tell you they vacuum their house once a week and take the trash to the curb every Thursday so we all agree that must qualify them for the job.

What about your company? What do you say to your new recruit that you just invested hundreds, maybe thousands of dollars in to find, interview, and put on the payroll?

"NOBODY EVER COMPLIMENTS ME"

This reason should come as no surprise. People working in the service business usually only hear about it when there is a problem. What about you? Is the only time you really communicate with your staff is when there is a problem?

In the building service business, the usual procedure is for a supervisor or manager to come to work and ask the questions, "Any complaints today? What problems am I going to be faced with tonight? Who isn't coming to work this evening? How many people won't come to work and not even call in?" Sound familiar?

Let me ask you, "When was the last time you went to work and made a conscious effort to compliment your staff on a job well done"? Today? Yesterday? Last week? Never? It's a jungle out there. True, but the compliment you give your employees today or tonight may be the only good thing they hear today. They may have spent the entire day fighting off creditors or arguing with a spouse or child. Try giving a compliment, you'll like it, and so will they.

Let me offer this suggestion. Why not create a file of your employee's birthdays and the anniversary date of their employment and make a conscious effort to call them or stop by their work station on those important dates and congratulate them? You don't have to spend a lot of time and for goodness sake, don't make it sound fake. You will be amazed how great it will make them feel---and you.

I am not suggesting you overlook the mistakes they make or the poor work they perform. You have to take the appropriate action when the occasion calls for you to do so. Just be conscious of the good work they do and let them know about it and recognize the important dates in their life.

I know of managers and supervisors who will pick up pizza on a Friday night and deliver it to a work crew if they have gone a week or so without a complaint on service or if no one was absent or if they performed a special project exceptionally well. Create your own reason for doing something along this line. Make it random. By the way, stay and enjoy the pizza with them. Amazing what it will do for strengthening your relationship with them.

"THERE DOESN'T APPEAR TO BE ANY ROOM FOR ADVANCEMENT WITH THE COMPANY"

This reason for leaving is really interesting. At the time that the GREAT employee is leaving a company because there is no place to advance, the employer is shouting to the world, "I can't find any good supervisors and managers". Sound familiar?

I have had countless owners of service companies ask me if I knew of any good managers they could recruit from anywhere in the country. Most of the time my answer is, "Yes, in your own organization". They really are there most of the time. We just need to locate them and then give them the training and opportunity to succeed.

I can remember many times in the "olden days" the excitement we all had when we landed a new large account that would require a substantial number of GREAT employees. After the celebration and we all came back to earth and reality set in, we faced the issue of where would the leadership come from that would manage that new piece of business.

Our next step was to make the rounds and talk with each of our current supervisory staff and ask them if they had anyone working with them that could fill the role. Know the answer? "We don't have one person that could do it". So we started trying to steal people from our competitors who also didn't have qualified management people. Why is it the supervisor you hire away from the competitor is always "more qualified" than your own supervisor? If that's true, what does that say about your training program?

After a while I began to realize what was really happening. Our supervisors told us they didn't have anyone worth promoting because if they let them go to another location, they would have to start all over training someone in that position which only increased the supervisors workload until they got someone new trained the way they wanted them trained.

That is when we began digging deeper into our organization for people to attend our quarterly management meetings which I will explain in greater detail in a later chapter. In this way, I became more knowledgeable as to who was in the ranks ready for promotion when the situation presented itself.

This reason that people leave companies is actually pretty easy to remedy but it will require top management's involvement every step of the way.

"NOBODY TRAINED ME"

This reason is a continuation of the first one where they said nobody told me what to do. The point here is that if they were told what to do, no one trained them on how to do it. Sound like someone you know? I certainly hope not.

When I talk about training, which will be discussed in greater detail in a later chapter, I am not talking about training where someone is hired and then sent out with a current employee to "learn the ropes". These may be the very ropes you would like to get rid of. That current employee may only show them a series of WRONG ways of doing what it is you want done. I am talking about a formal training program that teaches, in detail, your company's way of performing the tasks you assured your customer would be done in a professional manner. I personally believe that "on the job" training is a recipe for eventual disaster.

I know of many companies who justify on the job training by saying they want the new employee to see how it is really done out in the field. In most cases, that's the problem. It's being done WRONG out in the field if you don't have a formal training program and you only amplify the problem by sending new employees out to learn how to hang themselves with that rope you are wanting them to learn.

Create a training program, commit the resources to it and MAKE IT HAPPEN ASAP. You WILL see positive results.

I know of and have worked with companies that have focused their efforts on these 4 issues and have seen their turnover rates go from 325% down to as low as 40%. Most have settled in around the 75% number. To a professional organization such as a law firm or accounting firm, 75% may seem high and it may be to them, but if you are in the fast food or building service contracting business, having a turnover rate in this range is real progress in the grand scope of things.

Some companies have taken these four major reasons for turnover in the service business and framed them and put them in their Human Resource offices as well as all their manager's offices as a constant reminder to keep focused on why people leave service employment.

- ◆ Nobody told me what to do

- ◆ Nobody ever compliments me

- ◆ There is no room for advancement

- ◆ Nobody trained me

For those of you who think pay is important, and it is, it was next in line of why people leave coupled with lack of benefits.

I fully understand that pay is a very important issue and have always tried to keep it in focus as well as the other four. The reality is this… many times service employment such as contract cleaning, fast food, retail clerks and similar positions are considered entry level positions and pay will always be an issue UNTIL staff members are trained to a point that they can move up the ladder and make it a career as we have discussed in part 1 of this book. Career opportunities abound in the service sector but we need to tell that story and make the commitment to recruit and train a primary focus of our individual company's growth. The GREAT people are there, we have the responsibility to recruit and keep them.

In the meantime, I tried my best, not always successfully, to be at the top end of the pay scale for the positions I had in my company. We tried to be sure that if someone made our industry their career, we would be near the top in pay and benefits. Didn't always succeed, but we tried. Another position you want to put yourself in is to always try and have the best trained people. Believe me, this will pay dividends in the long run. Remember, we are offering careers, not just jobs.

Thought for the day: **The story is told about the legendary college basketball coach, Bobby Knight, that after a game where his team had played particularly bad and had lost a game they should have won, he was asked by the press what he thought of his team's execution? The story goes that Mr. Knight, without hesitation was said to have responded, "I'm all for it".**

-   Author Unknown

CHAPTER 11

THE ORIENTATION PROCESS

We have now reached the point where we want to begin to assimilate the new potentially GREAT employee into our organization. I submit to you that it is more than having them ride with Sue or Joe for a couple of days or nights. It should be an organized process assuring that each new GREAT employee hears the same thing in the same manner EVERY time. Not doing this only creates difficulty down the road when a question arises and finger pointing begins.

The balance of this chapter is devoted to various sample processes and procedures that may be helpful to you in the hiring process of GREAT employees for your company. I found it extremely beneficial to create a hiring process manual that outlined the steps and procedures I wanted followed in order to create the best company environment for a new GREAT team member.

As you review the contents of the information, please keep in mind that each company will need to change certain pieces of the process to comply with state law where they are located as well as any new federal law changes such as I-9 procedures, etc. that may have and probably have occurred since this writing.

Let me also emphasize that my company used the Team Cleaning process and you may not do so or choose to do so. Therefore you will need to substitute your system of cleaning, eliminating the various Team Cleaning Specialist positions I have outlined.

AS A PRECAUTION, LET ME REMIND YOU WE OFFER NO LEGAL ADVICE AND DO NOT GUARANTEE THAT THE INFORMATION CONTAINED IN THE HIRING PROCESS PROCEDURES SHOWN COMPLY WITH ALL LAWS. ATTEMPTS WERE MADE AT THE TIME THEY WERE DEVELOPED FOR THEM TO BE CORRECT BUT NO ABSOLUTE GUARANTEES CAN BE MADE. WE OFFER THEM AS ILLUSTRATIONS ONLY AND YOU SHOULD SEEK LEGAL AND FINANCIAL ADVICE PRIOR TO IMPLEMENTING ANY PROCEDURE OR POLICY.

The real issue here is that you have a systematic process for bringing new GREAT employees on board.

Included in the information that follows is:

- **Step 1 - Pre-Employment Application Packet**
- **Step 2 - Post-Hire Conditional Job Offer**
- **Step 3 - Receipt & Acknowledgment Packet to include employee confidentiality and Non-Compete Agreements**
- **Step 4 - The Actual Orientation Process**

CONSULTANTS IN CLEANING, LLC
HIRING PROCESS MANUAL

Disclaimer

Neither Consultants In Cleaning, LLC nor its legal counsel makes any representations as to the legality of the ideas or statements contained herein. Further, any bidding figures, cost estimates or prices are based upon hypothetical situations and are used solely for the purpose of illustration. All persons should consult with their own legal counsel concerning the many questions or problems that may arise.

Richard D. Ollek, CBSE

TABLE OF CONTENTS

HIRING PROCESS

Overview

Step 1: Pre Employment Application Packet
- Procedures
- Pre-Employment Application (Form _____)
- Job and Performance Descriptions (Form _____)
- Job Descriptions for the Light Duty Specialist, Vacuum Specialist, Restroom Specialist, and Utility Specialist

Step 2: Post-Hire Conditional Job Offer & Medical History Packet
- Procedures
- Post Hire Conditional Job Offer & Medical History (Form _____)
- Form W-4 (Current Year)
- Form I-9 (Employment Eligibility Verification)
- Medical Benefits Forms

Step 3: Receipt & Acknowledgment Packet
- Procedures
- Employee take home packet:
  - Welcome letter signed by *Your Company Representative*
  - You're Part of Our Team document
  - Employment Policies and Procedures Hand Book
  - Current year calendar of pay dates
  - Job and Performance Descriptions (Form _____)

- **Job Descriptions for the Light Duty Specialist, Vacuum Specialist, Restroom Specialist, and Utility Specialist**
- **Post-Hire Assignment Form (Form ____)**
- **Timekeeping Procedures Form**
- **Employee Confidentiality and Non-Compete Agreement (Form ____)**
- **Receipt & Acknowledgment document (Form ____)**

Step 4: Orientation
- **Procedures**
- **Description of Duties for:**
  - **Light Duty Specialist**
  - **Vacuum Specialist**
  - **Restroom Specialist**
  - **Utility Specialist**
  - **Floor Machine Specialist**
- **New-Hire Processing Checklist**

1. **Overview**

   1.1 (*Your Company Name*) **is looking for employees who:**

   1.1.1. Strive to deliver quality service in a genuine warm friendly manner.

   1.1.2. Are clean and neat in appearance.

   1.1.3. Possess a good team attitude.

   1.2 Putting a person on the (*Your Company Name*) **payroll is a four (4) step process.**

   1.0.1 Step 1 – Pre-Employment Application Packet

   1.0.2 Step 2 – Post-Hire Conditional Job Offer & Medical Review Packet

   1.0.3 Step 3 – Receipt & Acknowledgement packet (final paper processing)

   1.0.4 Step 4 – Orientation

   1.3 Federal and State laws require mandatory documentation which must be completed.

   1.1.1. W-4

   1.1.2. I-9

   1.3. (*Your Company Name*) **requires all employees to be trained in our cleaning process that creates a safe and efficient work environment**

   1.4. Use other language versions if needed and offer interpretation for understanding.

1. **Pre-Employment Process (step 1)**

    2.1. **All prospective employees are greeted in a friendly manner.**

    2.2. **No person will be denied employment based on age, sex, color, race, creed, national origin, religious persuasion, marital status, political belief, or disability that does not prohibit performance of essential job functions, nor will anyone receive special treatment for those reasons.**

    1.1. **All applicants are given the Pre-Employment Application Packet (*Your Company Name* Form ____) including the Job and Performance Descriptions.**

        2.3.1. **If applying for a cleaning technician job:**

        2.3.1.1 **Included with this Pre-Employment Application (Form ____) should be the cleaning technician Job and Performance Descriptions (*Your Company Name* Form ____) & Job Descriptions for each specialist.**

            1.1.2.0.1. **Light Duty Specialist**

            1.1.2.0.2. **Vacuum Specialist**

            1.1.2.0.3. **Restroom Specialist**

            1.1.2.0.4. **Utility Specialist**

            1.1.2.0.5. **Floor Machine Specialist**

            1.1.2.1. **If applying for a job other than a cleaning technician, attach the appropriate job and performance description to the Pre-Employment Application.**

1.2. You may make available to the applicant our Employment Policies and Procedures Handbook and other information about *Your Company Name*. It is strongly suggested that *Your Company Name* offices contain wall and table displays with information about *Your Company Name* and the job descriptions. This material is not intended to be sent with the applicant, but hand-out material can be, if you wish.

2.5. Your decision as to offering a job to the applicant is based on the Pre-Employment Application, your background investigations, and your judgment. Select the best qualified to fill your requirements.

2.6. Make the offer.

2.7. After you have made the job offer, and the applicant has accepted, the post-hiring process starts.

2. Post-Hire Process (step 2)

3.1. Internal Revenue "Form W-4" (current year).

3.2. Immigration and Naturalization Service form "I-9, Employment Eligibility Verification (get from the employee).

    3.2.1. One document from list "A" in Form I-9.

    3.2.2. Or one document from list "B" and one document from list "C" in the Form I-9.

    3.2.3. Update as laws change.

    3.2.4. Make a copy of these documents for *Your Company Name* files.

3. **Receipt & Acknowledgment Process (step 3)**

   4.1. The following should be in the *Your Company Name* Representative's possession prior to processing the employee.

      4.1.1. The completed Pre-Employment Packet

      4.1.2. The Post-Hire Packet

      4.1.3. The Employee take home packet

         4.1.3.1. Includes the following:

            4.1.3.1.1. "Welcome to *Your Company Name*" letter (1 page)

            4.1.3.1.2. "You're Part of Our Team" letter (1 page)

            4.1.3.1.3. Employment Policies and Procedures handbook

            4.1.3.1.4. Current year calendar of pay dates

            4.1.3.1.5. Job and Performance Descriptions

            4.1.3.1.6. Job Descriptions for the Light Duty Specialist, Vacuum Specialist, Restroom Specialist, and Utility Specialist

            4.1.3.1.7. Post-Hire Assignment Form / *Your Company Name* Form _____ (1 page)

         4.1.4. Employee Confidentiality and Non-Compete Agreement (*Your Company Name* Form _____)

         4.1.5. Receipt & Acknowledgement document (*Your Company Name* Form _____)

4.1.6. The following should be offered:

4.1.6.1. Assistance for completion should be offered if needed.

4.1.6.2. Other language version should be used if needed.

4.2. Processing Procedures.

4.2.1. Give the employee a copy of the Job and Performance Description (*Your Company Name* keeps a copy with the application).

4.2.1.1. Make sure the block indicating receipt of a job description is marked "yes".

4.2.1.2. Use the "Receipt & Acknowledgement" document (2 pages) to verify completion of the Post-Hire packet.

4.2.1.2.1. The employee must sign, initial and check the appropriate blocks.

4.2.1.2.2. The *Your Company Name* Representative will sign and print the *Your Company Name* District in the appropriate places.

4.2.1.2.3. *Your Company Name* keeps the "Receipt & Acknowledgement" document (employee does not need a copy).

4.2.2. The Post-Hire Assignment Form (*Your Company Name* Form _____) will be filled out by the *Your Company Name* Representative

4.2.2.1. The original copy is given to the employee.

        4.2.2.2. The second original or a copy is kept by *Your Company Name*.

4. **Orientation (step 4)**

  5.1. **May be done one-on-one, or in a class setting.**

      5.1.1. **Should be completed prior to the employee going to the job site.**

      5.1.2. **Should be conducted in English or other language as the situation requires.**

  5.2. **Welcome each person to the class.**

      5.2.1. **Use the "Welcome Letter" and "You're Part of Our Team" letter as a guide.**

        5.2.1.1. **Give a brief history of *Your Company Name* and its locations with emphasis on your District.**

        5.2.1.2. **Show orientation video.**

        5.2.1.3. **Stress *Your Company Name* goals and teamwork.**

          5.2.1.3.1. **Reputation for quality service.**

          5.2.1.3.2. **Pride in your work.**

          5.2.1.3.3. **Treating people with respect and dignity.**

          5.2.1.3.4. **Stress each employee is a Professional.**

          5.2.1.3.5. **Stress each employee is responsible for their own actions and are held accountable.**

          5.2.1.3.6. **Stress good team attitude.**

4.1. Show the videos on each of the following to all employees. Then their specific job. In each case, explain safety, MSDS and chemicals used.

4.1.1. Light Duty Specialist

4.1.1.1. Show brute and proper lifting techniques.

4.1.1.2. Demonstrate glass cleaning techniques and chemicals.

4.1.1.3. Demonstrate carpet spotting and chemicals.

4.1.1.4. Advise that not all surfaces in the entire building are dusted each night, but on a rotation basis (Quad area cleaning).

4.1.2. Vacuum Specialist

4.1.2.1. Show backpack video (appropriate language).

4.1.2.2. Demonstrate proper way to put on and wear the backpack.

4.1.2.3. Demonstrate how to protect the cord from stress.

4.1.2.4. Demonstrate vacuuming style.

4.1.2.5. Demonstrate how to check the bags, filters, and emptying and cleaning procedures.

4.1.2.6. Have the employee empty the bag, remove and replace the filters.

4.1.2.7. Have the employee put on the backpack and adjust for proper fit and demonstrate vacuuming style.

4.1.2.8. Stress the importance of proper fit and safety.

4.1.2.9. Stress turning off lights and locking doors.

4.1.3. Restroom Specialist

4.1.3.1. Show video (appropriate language)

4.1.3.2. Give the handout titled Description of duties for Restroom Specialist

4.1.3.3. Review procedures and show chemicals and tools.

4.1.3.3.1. Stress eye protection and rubber glove use.

4.1.3.3.2. Show chemicals used.

4.1.3.3.3. Fill dispensers first (demonstrate).

4.1.3.3.4. Show sweeping techniques.

4.1.3.3.5. Clean fixtures and glass.

4.1.3.3.6. Show toothbrush and use.

4.1.3.3.7. Show wall, partition and door cleaning techniques.

4.1.3.3.8. Mopping techniques.

4.1.4. Utility Specialist

4.1.4.1. Show video (appropriate language).

4.1.4.2. Give the handout titled Description of duties for Utility Specialist.

4.1.4.2.1. Demonstrate lifting techniques for trash removal.

4.1.4.2.2. Demonstrate chemicals for the use of glass and metal cleaners.

4.1.4.2.3. Demonstrate Vacuum Specialist duties as this is the preferred method of sweeping certain hard surface floors.

4.1.4.2.4. Demonstrate dust and wet mopping and chemicals used.

4.1.4.2.5. Review staircase cleaning.

4.1.4.2.6. Demonstrate use of buffing machine if the job assigned requires the use.

4.1.5. Floor Machine Specialist

5.3.5.1 Show video (appropriate language).

4.1.5.2.1. Stripping and Recoating.

4.1.5.2.2. Carpet Cleaning.

4.1.5.1. Show and demonstrate the equipment to be used.

4.1.5.2. Review chemicals and the process for application.

4.2. Quick overview of the Employee Handbook.

4.2.1. Attendance and Punctuality (attendance bonus).

4.2.1.1. Proper timekeeping procedures.

4.2.1.1.1. Signing in.

4.2.1.1.2. Signing out.

4.2.1.2. If you're sick, call in 5 hours prior to start of your shift.

4.2.2. Review the pay periods and paydays.

4.2.3. Emphasize wearing of uniform and badges on each shift.

4.2.3.1. Issue Uniforms.

4.2.3.2. Issue ID badges.

4.2.4. Breakage policy:

4.2.4.1. Importance of being careful to protect property.

4.2.4.2. Do not take anything on or in desks or elsewhere.

4.2.4.3. Report all breakage.

4.2.4.4. 50/50 policy.

4.2.5. Explain the benefits:

4.2.5.1. Vacation & Holiday policy.

4.2.5.2. Group Insurance (over 30 hours/week).

4.2.5.3. Payroll Insurance Deduction Plan.

4.2.6. Sexual Harassment will not be tolerated:

4.2.6.1. We have an anonymous hot line (1-800-000-0000 Ext. 000)

4.2.6.2. Use hot line for any reason.

4.2.7. Drug and Alcohol Awareness (Drug Free Workplace)

4.2.7.1. Applicant testing.

4.2.7.2. For-cause testing.

4.2.7.3. Post-accident testing.

4.2.8. Explain rules of conduct.

4.2.9. Review vehicle policy and guidelines.

4.3. Review Safety.

4.3.1. Stress the importance of safety:

4.3.1.1. Lifting

4.3.1.1.1. If something is too heavy, don't attempt to lift or move it without help.

4.3.1.1.2. Lifting belts.

4.3.1.2. Slip and Falls

4.3.1.2.1. Use safety signs when working on wet floors.

4.3.1.2.2. Wear rubber sole shoes (unless your job site requires different foot wear).

4.3.1.3. Use of rubber gloves and eye protection

4.3.1.3.1. Mandatory in restrooms.

4.3.1.3.2. Selected job sites may vary.

4.3.1.4. Hazard communication program (MSDS)

4.3.1.4.1. Location in building.

4.3.1.4.2. Necessity of labeling bottles (each bottle must have a label).

4.4. Questions and Answers.

4.4.1. Final Welcome to the TEAM.

4.4.2. Company news is distributed in newsletter.

4.4.2.1. Input for newsletter is encouraged.

4.4.2.2. All training classes are announced monthly. Plan to attend class that enhances your professionalism.

STEP 1
PRE EMPLOYMENT APPLICATION
PACKET

Includes:

<u>Procedures for Step 1</u>

1. Pre-Employment Application / *Your Company Name* Form _____ (2 pages)

2. Job and Performance Descriptions / *Your Company Name* Form _____

3. Job Descriptions for Light Duty Specialist, Vacuum Specialist, Restroom Specialist, and Utility Specialist

PROCEDURES FOR STEP 1

Pre-Employment Process (step 1)

1. All prospective employees are greeted in a friendly manner.

2. No person will be denied employment based on age, sex, color, race, creed, national origin, religious persuasion, marital status, political belief, or disability that does not prohibit performance of essential job functions, nor will anyone receive special treatment for those reasons.

3. All applicants are given the Pre-Employment Application Packet (*Your Company Name* Form ____) including the Job and Performance Descriptions.

   - If applying for a cleaning technician job:

     o Included with this Pre-Employment Application (Form ____) should be the cleaning technician Job and Performance Descriptions (*Your Company Name* Form ____), & Job Titles and Descriptions (*Your Company Name* Form ____) which includes the 5 specialists.

       ♦ Light Duty Specialist

       ♦ Vacuum Specialist

       ♦ Restroom Specialist

◆ **Utility Specialist**

◆ **Floor Machine Specialist**

- If applying for a job other than a cleaning technician, attach the appropriate job and performance description to the Pre-Employment Application.

4. You may make available to the applicant our Employment Policies and Procedures Handbook (see Step 3) and other information about *Your Company Name*. It is strongly suggested that *Your Company Name* offices contain wall and table displays with information about *Your Company Name* and the job descriptions. This material is not intended to be sent with the applicant, but hand-out material can be, if you wish.

5. Your decision as to offering a job to the applicant is based on the Pre-Employment Application, your background investigations, and your judgment. Select the best qualified to fill your requirements.

6. Make the job offer.

7. After you have made the job offer, and the applicant has accepted, the post-hiring process starts (see Step 2).

Richard D. Ollek, CBSE

```
┌─────────────────────┐
│                     │
│ Your Company Logo   │
│ Here                │
│                     │
└─────────────────────┘
```

PRE-EMPLOYMENT APPLICATION

NOTICE TO APPLICANTS

If you need help to fill out this application form, or for any phase of the employment process, please notify the person that gave you this form and every effort will be made to accommodate your needs in a reasonable amount of time.

1. Complete both pages of this form.
2. If more space is needed to complete any question, please attach a separate piece of paper.
3. Print clearly. Incomplete or illegible applications will not be processed.

PERSONAL DATA

TODAY'S DATE:_____

NAME:_____
       LAST   FIRST   M.I.

SOCIAL SECURITY NUMBER:_____

HOME PHONE:_____ WORK PHONE:_____

CURRENT ADDRESS:_____
                 STREET   COUNTY
CITY/STATE/ZIP:_____
                 CITY   STATE   ZIP

PREVIOUS ADDRESS:_____
                  STREET   COUNTY
CITY/STATE/ZIP:_____

PREVIOUS ADDRESS:_____
                  STREET   COUNTY
CITY/STATE/ZIP:_____

AVAILABILITY

For which position are you applying? Please check all that apply. See attached pages for job descriptions.

☐ **LIGHT DUTY SPECIALIST**   ☐ **RESTROOM SPECIALIST**   ☐ **FLOOR MACHINE SPECIALIST**

☐ **VACUUM SPECIALIST**   ☐ **UTILITY SPECIALIST**   ☐ **OTHER (PLEASE SPECIFY)**

Which time range are you available?   What category would you prefer?   Date available to start work
☐ Weekdays   ☐ Full-time (6-8 hrs per day)   _____
☐ Evenings   ☐ Part-time (3-4 hrs per day)
☐ Nights
☐ Weekends   **ALL SHIFT TIMES ARE APPROXIMATE AND ARE SUBJECT TO CHANGE.**

SECURITY

Have you used any names or Social Security Numbers other than those on this page? If yes, please list: ☐ Yes   ☐ No
_____

1. Have you been convicted of a crime involving theft (such as shoplifting, robbery, burglary, credit card fraud, check fraud, embezzlement) or a drug related crime?
☐ Yes ☐ No
2. Have you been convicted of a crime of violence (such as assault, battery, use/possession of a deadly weapon, a sexual offense, stalking)? ☐ Yes ☐ No
3. Have you stipulated to or admitted to the commission of a crime in a court proceeding for a crime involving theft (such as shoplifting, robbery, burglary, credit card fraud, check fraud, embezzlement) or a drug related crime? ☐ Yes ☐ No
4. Have you been convicted of a felony, or plea bargained from a felony charge to a misdemeanor? ☐ Yes ☐ No
5. Have you ever been discharged by an employer due to a theft related incident, situation involving dishonesty or a crime involving theft (such as shoplifting, misappropriation of property, robbery, burglary, credit card fraud, check fraud, embezzlement) or a drug related crime? ☐ Yes ☐ No
6. Have you ever been disciplined or discharged by an employer for sexual harassment? ☐ Yes ☐ No
If you answered "Yes" to questions 1 through 6, write the details on the back of this page.

JOB-RELATED SKILLS   **NOTE:** Do not fill out any part of the following section you believe to be non-job related.

Foreign Languages 1. _____	☐ Read ☐ Write ☐ Speak
2. _____	☐ Read ☐ Write ☐ Speak

If the job requires, do you have the appropriate valid drivers license?	☐ Yes	☐ No
DL#_____ Type_____ State of issue_____		
Have you had any moving violations?	☐ Yes	☐ No
Please describe_____		
Have you been given a job description or had the requirements of the job explained to you?	☐ Yes	☐ No
Do you understand these requirements?	☐ Yes	☐ No
Can you perform the requirements of this job without accommodation?	☐ Yes	☐ No
If you answered "No", what accommodations are necessary?_____		

Your Company Name Form ____
Revised Effective _____

LAST NAME _____ FIRST NAME _____

EMPLOYMENT EXPERIENCE

PLEASE NOTE. Your application will not be considered unless every question in this section is answered. Since we will make every effort to contact previous employers, the *correct telephone numbers of past employers are critical.* If you need assistance, please ask.

Current (or Last) Employer	Street Address	City, State	Zip Code	Telephone
Job Title	Description of Duties		Supervisor's Name	
From Mo. Yr. To Mo. Yr. ___ __ / __ __ __ __ / __ __	Start Salary	Final Salary	Reason for Leaving	May We Contact Current Employer? ☐ Yes ☐ No
Previous Employer	Street Address	City, State	Zip Code	Telephone
Job Title	Description of Duties		Supervisor's Name	
From Mo. Yr. To Mo. Yr. ___ __ / __ __ __ / __	Start Salary	Final Salary	Reason for Leaving	
Previous Employer	Street Address	City, State	Zip Code	Telephone
Job Title	Description of Duties		Supervisor's Name	
From Mo. Yr. To Mo. Yr. ___ __ / __ __ __ / __	Start Salary	Final Salary	Reason for Leaving	
Previous Employer	Street Address	City, State	Zip Code	Telephone
Job Title	Description of Duties		Supervisor's Name	
From Mo. Yr. To Mo. Yr. ___ __ / __ __ __ / __	Start Salary	Final Salary	Reason for Leaving	

REFERENCES (Not a Relative)

NAME	ADDRESS/PHONE	YEARS KNOWN/RELATIONSHIP
1.		
2.		

APPLICANT NOTE

False statements = termination: Please answer all appropriate questions completely and accurately. False information, omissions or misrepresentations of facts, or misleading statements during the interview or on this application may result in rejection of my application or discharge if discovered at any time during employment.

Not a contract: This application form is intended for use in evaluating your qualifications for employment. This is not an employment contract.

Policy changes: The employment policies and procedures serve as a guide to personnel. *Your Company Name* reserves the right to change any policies at any time, for any reason, with or without notice. *Your Company Name* also reserves the right to make final decisions concerning the interpretation and revision of policies and procedures.

Employment at Will Agreement: I agree that, if hired, I will conform to the rules and regulations of *Your Company Name*, and further understand and agree that my employment is for no definite period and may, regardless of the time and manner of payment of my wages and salary, be terminated at any time by *Your Company Name* or me, with or without cause or any previous notice. Further, I understand that no District Manager or Representative of *Your Company Name* has the authority to enter into an agreement for employment for any specific period of time or to make any agreement contrary to the foregoing.

Equal opportunity employment: All qualified applicants will receive consideration without discrimination because of sex, marital status, race, age, creed, national origin or the presence of disabilities.

Felony conviction: A felony conviction will not necessarily bar an applicant from employment.

Affirmative Action Questionnaire: This information is being gathered for Affirmative Action under section 503 of the Rehabilitation Act of 1973. This information requested is voluntary and will be kept confidential. An applicant will not be subject to any adverse treatment for refusing to complete the questionnaire.

Drug & other testing: Additional testing of job related skills and for the presence of drugs in your body may be required prior to employment.

Medical history: After an offer of employment, and prior to reporting to work, you will be required to complete a medical history form and may be **required** to be examined by a medical professional designated by the company.

CERTIFICATION AND RELEASE

Authorization for release of information: I authorize the company and/or its agents, including consumer reporting bureaus, to verify any of this information including, but not limited to, criminal history and motor vehicle driving records. I authorize all persons, schools, companies and law enforcement authorities to release any information concerning my background and hereby release any said persons, schools, companies and law enforcement authorities from any liability for any damage whatsoever for issuing this information.

Illegal drug use: I also understand that the use of illegal drugs is prohibited during employment. I am willing to submit to drug testing to detect the use of illegal drugs prior to and during employment.

SIGNATURE	DATE

THIS APPLICATION WILL RECEIVE ACTIVE CONSIDERATION FOR 30 DAYS

Your Company Name Form _____
Revised Effective _____
Page 2 of 2

JOB AND PERFORMANCE DESCRIPTIONS

LIGHT DUTY SPECIALIST, VACUUM SPECIALIST, RESTROOM SPECIALIST, UTILITY SPECIALIST, FLOOR MACHINE SPECIALIST

All cleaning specialist jobs require the following qualifications

SPECIFIED RESPONSIBILITIES:

1. Perform cleaning duties at a maximum quality level.

2. Perform work within production time budgets and supply budgets.

3. Keep equipment clean and in good operating condition.

4. Follow all safety rules and participate in company's safety program.

5. Project a professional image and maintain good customer and public relations.

6. Adhere to company rules, policies, and operating procedures.

7. Reports to the site supervisor any equipment breakdowns, unsafe conditions, customer complaints and any other problems that may occur.

8. Adhere to tardiness and absenteeism policy.

9. Be able to work schedule as assigned by supervisor at various locations.

JOB AND PERFORMANCE DESCRIPTIONS

LIGHT DUTY SPECIALIST, VACUUM SPECIALIST, RESTROOM SPECIALIST, UTILITY SPECIALIST, FLOOR MACHINE SPECIALIST

All cleaning specialist jobs require the following qualifications

QUALIFICATION REQUIREMENTS:

To perform this successfully, an individual must be able to perform each essential duty satisfactorily. The requirements listed below are representative of the knowledge, skill and/or ability required. Reasonable accommodations may be made to enable individuals with disabilities to perform the essential functions.

Must have dependable transportation or be able to get to the job site scheduled.

LANGUAGE SKILLS:

Ability to read a limited number of two and three syllable words and to recognize similarities and differences between words and between series of numbers. Ability to print and speak simple sentences in English.

REASONING ABILITY:

Ability to apply common-sense understanding to carry out simple one- or two-step instructions. Ability to deal with standardized situations with only occasional or no variables.

Richard D. Ollek, CBSE

JOB AND PERFORMANCE DESCRIPTIONS

LIGHT DUTY SPECIALIST, VACUUM SPECIALIST, RESTROOM SPECIALIST, UTILITY SPECIALIST, FLOOR MACHINE SPECIALIST

All cleaning specialist jobs require the following qualifications

PHYSICAL DEMANDS:

The physical demands described here are representative of those which must be met by an employee to successfully perform the essential functions of the job.

Must be able to perform manual tasks requiring strength and to be in good physical health.

While performing the duties of the job, the employee is regularly required to reach with hands and arms. The employee continually is required to stand, walk, stoop, kneel, crouch and bend. The employee is repetitively required to use hands and fingers, to handle objects and equipment, to push and pull, to climb and balance, and to talk and hear. The employee must repeatedly lift and/or move up to 50 pounds. Specific vision abilities required by this job include close vision, distance vision, color vision, peripheral vision, depth perception, and the ability to adjust focus.

WORK ENVIRONMENT:

The work environment characteristics described here are representative of that an employee encounters while performing the essential functions of this job. Reasonable accommodations may be made to enable individuals with disabilities to perform the essential functions. While performing the duties of this job, the employees occasionally work near moving mechanical parts and are occasionally exposed to toxic or caustic chemicals, risk of electric shock, and vibration. The noise level in the work environment is usually moderate.

While this job description is intended to be an accurate reflection of the job requirements, management reserves the right to modify, add or remove duties from particular jobs and to assign other duties as necessary.

STEP 2

POST-HIRE CONDITIONAL JOB OFFER

& MEDICAL HISTORY PACKET

Includes:

<u>Procedures for Step 2</u>

1. Post-Hire Conditional Job Offer & Medical History / *Your Company Name* Form _____ (2 pages)

2. Form W-4 (current year)

3. Form I-9 (Employment Eligibility Verification)

4. Medical Benefits Forms

Procedures for Step 2

Post-Hire Process (step 2)

The Post-Hire Packet should include:

1. Post-Hire Conditional Job Offer & Medical History / Your Company Name Form ____.

2. Internal Revenue "Form W-4" (current year).

3. Immigration and Naturalization Service Form "I-9", Employment Eligibility Verification (get from the employee).

   - One document from list "A" in Form I-9.

   - Or one document from list "B" and one document from list "C" in the Form I-9.

   - Update as laws change.

   - Make a copy of these documents for Your Company Name files.

4. Medical Benefits Forms

   - Employee must fill out enrollment form (appropriate language) whether choosing to take or waive the medical insurance. The completed form must be faxed to the Corporate office.

POST-HIRE CONDITIONAL JOB OFFER & MEDICAL HISTORY

Applicant NOTE: This form is to be completed *only* after you have been given an offer of employment.

_____ _____ _____
APPLICANT NAME   POSITION OFFERED   DATE OF JOB OFFER

Based on qualifications presented on your application form and/or in your job interview, you are hereby offered a job **with *Your Company Name*** conditional upon submitting to our standard medical review and the verification of your answers to the following questions. Your job offer cannot and will not be rescinded unless a medical review reveals that you cannot perform the essential functions of the job (with accommodations if requested), or you present a hazard to yourself or others. False or misleading statements are also grounds for rescinding this offer. This form must be accurate and complete for us to process. This information is considered personal and medical in nature and will be treated as such by handling it confidentially in strict compliance with the Americans with Disabilities Act (ADA). This offer is valid only if the back of this page is signed by a *Your Company Name* representative.

EMERGENCY INSTRUCTIONS

In case of emergency, contact: _____ _____
                              NAME   PHONE NUMBER

_____ _____ _____ _____
STREET   CITY   STATE   ZIP

Are there any other emergency instructions, circumstances, medical needs, allergic responses or procedures *Your Company Name* should know?

_____

_____

(Continue in COMMENTS SECTION on back if necessary.)

HEALTH AND SAFETY

I. ☐ Yes   ☐ No   Have you had any injuries on the job?

If yes, please describe:

	First injury	Second injury	Third injury
a) date of injury			
b) employer			
c) body part affected			
d) cause			
e) amount of lost time			
f) any permanent disability (%)?			
g) was worker's comp claim filed?			

Please list any others in COMMENTS SECTION on page 2

II. ☐ Yes   ☐ No   Do you have or have you had other injuries or illnesses not on the job (home, auto, sports, hunting, etc.) that have resulted in hospitalization, surgery or lost work time?

If yes, please describe:

	First occurrence	Second occurrence	Third occurrence
a) date of injury/illness			
b) body part affected			
c) cause			
d) days in hospital			
e) days lost work time			
f) have you recovered?			

Please list any others in COMMENT SECTION on the back

YOUR COMPANY NAME Form _____
Revised Effective _____
Page 1 of 2

Richard D. Ollek, CBSE

APPLICANT NAME _____ **POSITION OFFERED** _____

III. ☐ Yes   ☐ No   Are you taking any long term (more than 30 days) prescribed medications?

If yes, please describe:
  a) type of medication
  b) purpose
  c) side effects

1	2	3

IV. ☐ Yes   ☐ No   Do you have or have you been diagnosed as having any illness or injury for
which you are not seeking treatment?

If yes, please describe:

_____
_____
_____
_____

COMMENTS

_____
_____
_____
_____

AFFIRMATION AND AUTHORIZATION

I hereby affirm that the information on this form is true and correct, and that there are no omissions. I authorize any physician, medical facility, law enforcement agency, administrator, state agency, institution, information service bureau, insurance company or employer contacted by this company or an agent of this company to furnish or verify worker's compensation information and medical records.

I further acknowledge that a telephone facsimile (FAX) or photographic copy shall be as valid as the original.

_____
Today's date   Signature of Applicant

_____
Today's date   Authorized Signature of *Your Company Name* Representative

You will be given *Your Company Name* Form ___, Post-Hire Assignment Form for job assignment and starting pay.

FOR *YOUR COMPANY NAME* USE ONLY

_____
_____
_____
_____

STEP 3
RECEIPT & ACKNOWLEDGMENT
PACKET

(Final paper processing)

Includes:

Procedures for Step 3

1. *Your Company Name* Representative/Trainer gives employee "Employee Take Home Packet" which includes the following:

    - Welcome letter (1 page)

    - You're Part of Our Team document (1 page)

    - Employment Policies and Procedures handbook

    - Current year calendar of pay dates

    - Job and Performance Descriptions / *Your Company Name* Form ____

- Job Descriptions for the Light Duty Specialist, Vacuum Specialist, Restroom Specialist, and Utility Specialist

- Post-Hire Assignment Form / *Your Company Name* Form _____

2. *Your Company Name* Representative / Trainer has employee (if hired as District Manager, Area Manager, Area Supervisor, Site Supervisor, Project Manager, Team Leader, Warehouse / Delivery Person, Administrative Assistant, or any Corporate position) read "Employee Confidentiality and Non-Compete Agreement".

  - Have the employee sign where indicated

  - *Your Company Name* Representative / Trainer signs where indicated

  - Fax copy to *Your Company Name* Corporate office

3. *Your Company Name* Representative / Trainer reviews all items in #1 above with employee. Use the Receipt & Acknowledgment document (*Your Company Name* Form _____) as your guide.

  - Have the employee sign and initial where indicated

  - *Your Company Name* Representative / Trainer signs where indicated

  - *Your Company Name* Representative / Trainer prints District name at lower right side of each page

4. *Your Company Name* retains the Receipt & Acknowledgement document (*Your Company Name* Form _____) (Employee does not need this unless they request a copy).

5. Fax a copy to *Your Company Name* Corporate office.

Procedures for Step 3

Receipt & Acknowledgment Process (step 3)

The following should be in the *Your Company Name* Representative's possession prior to processing the employee.

1. The completed Pre-Employment Packet.

2. The Post-Hire Packet.

3. The Employee Take Home Packet. Includes the following:

    - "Welcome to *Your Company Name*" letter (1 page).

    - "You're Part of Our Team" letter (1 page).

    - Employment Policies and Procedures Handbook.

    - Current year calendar of pay dates.

    - Job and Performance Descriptions / *Your Company Name* Form _____.

    - Job Descriptions for the Light Duty Specialist, Vacuum Specialist, Restroom Specialist, and Utility Specialist.

    - Post-Hire Assignment Form / *Your Company Name* Form _____.

4. Employee Confidentiality and Non-Compete Agreement (*Your Company Name* Form _____).

5. Receipt & Acknowledgment Document (*Your Company Name* Form _____).

6. The following should be offered:

- Assistance for completion should be offered if needed.

- Use other language version if needed.

Processing Procedures.

1. Give the employee a copy of the Job and Performance Description (*Your Company Name* keeps a copy with the application).

   - Make sure the block indicating receipt of job description is marked "yes".

   - Use the "Receipt and Acknowledgment" document" to verify completion of the Post-Hire packet.

   - The employee must sign, initial and check the appropriate blocks.

   - The *Your Company Name* Representative will sign and print the *Your Company Name* District in the appropriate places.

   - *Your Company Name* keeps the "Receipt & Acknowledgement" document (employee does not need a copy).

2. The Post-Hire Assignment Form (*Your Company Name* Form ___) will be filled out by the *Your Company Name* Representative.

   - The original copy is given to the employee.

   - The second original or a copy is kept by *Your Company Name.*

Welcome to
YOUR COMPANY NAME

Dear Team Member:

We are very happy to welcome you to *Your Company Name.* Thank you for joining us! We want you to feel that your association with *Your Company Name* will be mutually beneficial and pleasant.

You have joined an organization that has established an outstanding reputation for quality services. Credit for this goes to every one of our employees. We hope you, too, will find satisfaction and take pride in your work here.

Our Employment Policies and Procedures Hand Book provides answers to most of the questions you may have about *Your Company Name*'s benefit programs, as well as the company policies and procedures we abide by -- our responsibilities to you and your responsibilities to *Your Company Name.* If anything is unclear, please discuss the matter with your manager. You are responsible for reading, (or having read to you) and understanding the Employment Policies and Procedures Handbook. In addition to clarifying responsibilities, we hope these documents also give you an indication of *Your Company Name's* interest in the welfare of all who work here. If you wish to contact me about any concern, I offer a toll-free anonymous hot line. Please call 1-800-000-0000 Ext. 000 at any time.

Compensation and personal satisfaction gained from doing a job well are only some of the reasons most people work. Most likely, many other factors count among your reasons for working -- pleasant relationships and working conditions, career development and promotion opportunities, and health benefits are just a few. *Your Company Name* is committed to doing its part to assure you of a satisfying work experience.

I extend to you my personal best wishes for your success and happiness at *Your Company Name*

Sincerely yours,

YOUR COMPANY NAME

You're Part of Our Team...

As a member of **Your Company Name's** team, you will be expected to contribute your talents and energies to improve the environment and quality of the company, as well as the company's services to its customers. In return, you will be given opportunities to grow and advance in your career.

Your Company Name is dedicated to two standards:

1. To provide our customers with the best quality services at competitive prices that in turn produces a profit for our company.

2. To provide you with wages and benefits comparable to others doing similar work within the industry and within the region.

At **Your Company Name**, we always put safety first. We believe it is our duty to provide you with as safe a workplace as possible. For your protection, we have an in-house safety inspection program and we enlist the services of outside safety consulting representatives. We also have a policy concerning substance abuse to promote a drug-free workplace, because you have a right to know you can depend on your co-workers and they can depend on you.

The only things we require for employment, compensation, advancement, and benefits are performance and a good team attitude. However, all employment at **Your Company Name** is "at will." No one will be denied opportunities or benefits on the basis of age, sex, color, race, creed, national origin, religious persuasion, marital status, political belief, or disability that does not prohibit performance of essential job functions; nor will anyone receive special treatment for those reasons.

No employee manual can answer every question, nor would we want to restrict the normal question and answer interchange among us. It is in our person-to-person conversations that we can better know each other, express our views, and work together in a harmonious relationship.

Richard D. Ollek, CBSE

We hope our Employment Policies and Procedures Handbook will help you feel comfortable with us. We depend on you -- your success is our success. Please don't hesitate to ask questions. Your manager will gladly answer them. We believe you will enjoy your work and your fellow employees here. We also believe you will find ***Your Company Name*** a good place to work.

YOUR COMPANY NAME

IS AN EQUAL OPPORTUNITY EMPLOYER

EMPLOYMENT POLICIES
AND PROCEDURES

**A warm and friendly welcome to you
as a new *Your Company Name* employee.**

Revised Effective _____

CORPORATE MISSION STATEMENT

(Include your company's mission statement here)

ATTENDANCE AND PUNCTUALITY

In order to give the best possible service to **Your Company Name** customers, it is important for all employees to arrive at work regularly and to be on time. We realize that emergencies such as sickness, death in the family, accidents, etc., do occur. If such an emergency arises, you must call in at least 5 hours prior to the start of your shift. Communication between employees, supervisors, and managers after 5:00 p.m. is done primarily through the use of tone pagers. When using the pager system, enter your phone number from where you are calling and your call will be returned. If your call is not returned within 15 minutes, please call again.

WORKING HOURS AND LOCATION

Your Supervisor will outline working hours for your particular work assignment. There is no deviation from such an assignment without your Immediate Supervisor's approval. You must understand that as a part-time or full-time employee, we cannot guarantee the same hours every week, and your hours may vary from week to week. You must also understand that your assigned location and assigned shift are also subject to change, and that you are responsible for your own transportation to and from work. From time to time you may be given the opportunity to temporarily work increased hours. However, if you do accept additional hours, you must understand that this will not be construed as a permanent change in hours. **Your Company Name** reserves the right to transfer and assign employees to new jobs or building locations as best serves the needs of **Your Company Name**. In the event that an assignment should come to an end, it is your responsibility to contact **Your Company Name** for reassignment as soon as possible.

BREAKS

For employees who work less than 6 hours per shift, no breaks are authorized. For employees who work 6 to 8 hours per shift, 1/2 hour lunch break is mandatory. Breaks are not paid. All breaks must be confined to the specific break area. Smoking, eating, etc. is not permitted while working but will be allowed in break areas only.

AUTOMATED TIME AND ATTENDANCE POLICY

The purpose of the Time and Attendance system is to ensure that all employees are paid accurately and timely. This system will also help provide accountability for the employee and help ***Your Company Name*** to contact the employee in case of emergencies.

It is the personal responsibility of each ***Your Company Name*** employee to call the system (from a pre-assigned phone within each job site) and check in at the start of their shift, check out and back in for authorized breaks, and check out at the end of their shift.

NON-AUTOMATED TIME AND ATTENDANCE POLICY

All employees working in areas that are not on the automated time system are to sign themselves in at the start of their shift, sign out and back in for authorized breaks, and sign themselves out at the end of their shift on ***Your Company Name*** timekeeping registers.

Under no circumstances is an employee to sign any other employee in or out for their shift. Failure of any employee to follow these instructions will result in the employee receiving disciplinary action up to and including discharge.

PAYDAY

Payday procedures will be explained during orientation. Our work week runs Sunday through Saturday. On payday you may pick up your check between 8:00 a.m. and 5:00 p.m., or you can have it mailed. If at any time you change your address, please notify the ***Your Company Name*** district office in your area so your check and correspondence can be mailed to your correct address.

NON-DISCLOSURE OF CONFIDENTIAL INFORMATION

During the term of the employee's employment or afterwards, unless authorized in writing by ***Your Company Name***, the employee shall not disclose any Confidential Information, proprietary information, or trade secrets to any person nor shall the employee use the same for any purposes at any time, except for the purpose of performing the employee's job duties on behalf of or as directed by ***Your Company Name***. These include, but are not limited to, items such as schedules of maintenance, customer lists, proposals, all company manuals, training programs, pager and voice mail lists, production rates, etc.

TRAINING

Doing your job is vital to the growth of ***Your Company Name*** as well as your own opportunities for career growth. Many different methods of learning your job responsibilities are available through orientation, seminars, VCR films, company newsletter and company manuals to help expand your knowledge for future career opportunities. A schedule of upcoming seminars is published in the Company newsletter.

UNIFORMS AND DRESS CODE

It is mandatory that the employee be neat, clean, and in company uniform. Employees not wearing uniforms during working hours, will be subject to disciplinary action.

All employees are supplied with 3 shirts or smocks (if applicable). If you need to renew any items you should contact your Manager.

Safety clothing and equipment that are issued must be worn.

All uniforms are returnable when you leave our employ. Failure to return all uniforms will result in a deduction of $XX.XX from your last paycheck.

Long pants must be worn at all times except during the summer months, when navy or khaki walking shorts that reach the knees are permitted.

Tennis shoes or flat soled work shoes are mandatory. No high heeled shoes or sandals are allowed. Socks must be worn at all times.

The customer at the job site can override this uniform policy by what their safety and job site requirements are.

BREAKAGES

We would expect all **Your Company Name** employees to exercise the utmost care in handling our customer's and **Your Company Name's** property. When breakages do occur, our customers expect us to pay for the breakages. Therefore, in an attempt to promote carefulness, all breakages will be paid 1/2 by the employee and 1/2 by **Your Company Name**.

YOUR COMPANY NAME EQUIPMENT & SUPPLIES

All supplies, equipment, and tools are the property of **Your Company Name**. These products, equipment, and tools are to be used safely in accordance with the directions provided to the employee by their Manager. NO products, equipment, or tools are authorized to be used anywhere other than on **Your Company Name** job sites.

PROGRESSIVE DISCIPLINE

We make every effort to help employees achieve and maintain satisfactory performance. If it becomes necessary to discipline an employee, management is concerned with salvaging the employment relationship.

Discipline may be initiated with an employee for various reasons, including, but not limited to, violations of work rules or unsatisfactory performance. Decisions regarding appropriate discipline or termination are the sole judgment of management. Disciplinary action may take the form of verbal warnings, written warnings, suspension or discharge. The type of discipline imposed generally depends on the circumstances surrounding the violation, the nature of the offense, its effects on operations, and the employee's work record.

Written warnings will be included in the employee's personnel file.

RULES OF CONDUCT

It is management's belief that reasonable work rules are necessary to maintain an organized work setting, and to insure the efficient operation of our business.

The work rules listed below are intended to serve only as a guide. We recognize that it is not possible to list or define all of the policy violations that may occur. Management will consider the circumstances surrounding each individual offense and reserves the right to discharge for any reason at any time.

The following are examples of rule violations that may result in disciplinary action:

- Absenteeism and/or tardiness.
- Failure to follow electronic call in and/or timekeeping register procedures.
- Failure to follow Company safety rules or policies.
- Horseplay.
- Failure to follow dress code/uniform policies.
- Creating or contributing to an unsafe work environment.
- Discourtesy to co-workers or clients.
- Unauthorized breaks.
- Distracting co-workers or impeding co-worker performance.
- Poor job performance.
- Misuse of Company property or equipment.
- Using profanity or abrasive language.

Rule violations that may result in immediate discharge without warning include, but are not limited to:

- An employee that tests positive for an illegal or controlled substance or alcohol will be terminated.
- Falsification of Company records including calling in from unauthorized location(s).
- Failure to call or report for any scheduled shift.
- Drinking alcohol prior to, or during. your scheduled shift.
- Using illegal drugs prior to, or during, your scheduled shift.
- Possession, use, receipt, sale or distribution of alcohol or any illegal drug while on Company property, or property of a customer.
- Fighting or threatening a co-worker or customer.
- Stealing or attempting to steal the Company or the customers property.
- Possession of firearms or other weapons on Company property.
- Sleeping on the job.

- Insubordination.
- Any act of sexual harassment.
- Leaving during working hours without authorization.
- Failure to return to work following an authorized leave of absence.
- Failure to submit to or report for drug screening.

SEXUAL HARASSMENT

It is the policy of **Your Company Name** that sexual harassment of employees will not be tolerated. Sexual harassment includes unwelcome sexual advances, requests for sexual favors, and any other verbal, visual, or physical conduct of a sexual nature. Sexual harassment also includes unnecessary touching, sexually degrading words, sexually explicit and offensive jokes, or any display in the work place of sexually graphic objects or pictures.

Any employee who feels he/she is a victim of sexual harassment by any supervisor, manager, employee, or non-employee should bring the matter to the attention of his/her supervisor or area supervisor. An employee who is uncomfortable in bringing such a matter to the attention of his/her supervisor, or who is not satisfied after bringing the matter to the attention of his/her manager, should report the matter directly to our toll-free anonymous hot line 1-800-000-0000 Ext. 000.

The Company will promptly investigate all allegations of sexual harassment in as confidential a manner as possible, and appropriate action will be taken.

Any employee who is found in violation of this policy is subject to disciplinary action, up to and including immediate discharge.

VOLUNTARY RESIGNATION

We require that employees who elect to voluntarily resign from employment complete a resignation form, and we also require "proper notice." We consider "proper notice" to be not less than two weeks.

EXIT INTERVIEW

Employees resigning from the Company are encouraged to participate in an exit interview conducted by a member of the management staff.

The exit interview is an opportunity for separating employees to express their opinions concerning the management and operation of our business.

APPEALS

If, in your opinion, you were not treated fairly when a reprimand was issued or you wish to appeal a termination, the first appeal is to the Area Supervisor, then the Production Supervisor, and finally the District Manager. If needed, a final appeal can be made to the Vice President and/or to the President of the Company.

FINAL PAYCHECK

Whenever an employee terminates for any reason, or is terminated, all wages due after proper deductions will be paid on the next regular scheduled payday. Before issuing the final check however, all of *Your Company Name's* equipment and supplies such as (but not limited to) keys, uniforms, pagers, ID badges, manuals, etc. in the employee's possession must be returned.

During the term of the employee's employment or afterwards, unless authorized in writing by *Your Company Name*, the employee shall not disclose any Confidential Information, proprietary information, or trade secrets to any person nor shall the employee use the same for any purposes at any time, except for the purpose of performing the employee's job duties on behalf of or as directed by *Your Company Name*. These include, but are not limited to, items such as schedules of maintenance, customer lists, proposals, all company manuals, training programs, pager and voice mail lists, production rates, etc.

ATTENDANCE BONUS

All hourly employees whether full- or part-time who work 3 consecutive calendar months without missing a day of work (complete shift) will receive a bonus equal to one day's pay.

VACATION

Vacation benefits are provided to all full-time employees working 30 hours per week. The schedule is as follows:

> 1 week after 1 year of employment
> 2 weeks after 2 years of employment
> 3 weeks after 10 years of employment

In order to request vacation, an employee must fill out and return "The Request For Vacation" form to his or her immediate Supervisor thirty days prior to start of vacation.

GROUP INSURANCE

Health insurance protection is available to all full-time employees working 30 hours per week or more. You are eligible for this coverage 90 days after you are employed. Your coverage begins on the 1st of the month following completion of the 90 days. If you want this coverage you should notify the ***Your Company Name*** office within the first 60 days after you are employed.

Your Company Name's policy for health insurance coverage is that ***Your Company Name*** will pay for 50% of the employees monthly premium. The employee may add their spouse or children to the plan, however, the employee must pay 100% of their coverage.

If the employee elects to have coverage, they must complete the "***Optional Employee Deductible Selection Form***". If the employee elects to have coverage but not for their dependents, the "***Waiver of Dependent Coverage***" must be completed. These forms can be obtained in the district office.

If the employee elects not to sign up, the employee must complete the "***Non-Participating Employee Waiver***" form. If at a later date the employee decides they want to sign up for the health insurance program the next enrollment date would be May of the following year.

A complete schedule of benefits including hospitalization, major medical, life insurance, accidental death and dismemberment are included in a separate booklet available for each employee at the ***Your Company***

Name office. The benefits and costs under this policy can be explained in full by the insurance agent at your request for those wanting to become participants through our group plan.

You, as an employee, have the option to enroll in the insurance program or waive (refuse) coverage by initialing and signing the proper statement on the document titled "Receipt & Acknowledgment of *Your Company Name*, Employment Policies and Procedures Handbook".

HOLIDAYS - FULL TIME EMPLOYEES

Your Company Name observes the following six holidays which we also pay to all full-time employees who work 30 hours a week or more. You are eligible for holiday pay if you have been employed 180 days or more and work the shift before and the shift after the holiday. The holidays are:

1. **New Year's Day**   4. **Labor Day**
2. **Memorial Day**   5. **Thanksgiving**
3. **July 4th**   6. **Christmas**

* * *   Supervisors full- or part-time who control 24 (twenty-four) hours or more per day (include yourself) are eligible for the same benefits as full-time employees (30 hours or more per week).

HAZARD COMMUNICATION TRAINING

At the time of orientation the employee will receive training on *Your Company Name's* Hazard Communication Program (HazMat). Your training will include the following:

1. The purpose of the Hazard Communication Program.
2. The use of the Material Safety Data Sheets (MSDS).
3. The location of the Hazard Communication Program and MSDS's at the job site.

4. Product use and handling instructions for all products I use.
5. The use of personal protective equipment as required.
6. Emergency procedures in case of injury or spills.
7. The General Chemical Safety Handling rules.

The employee will abide by all safety rules indicated and required by **Your Company Name**, the client, and for any governing authority. The employee agrees to report any injury, spill or leak to their immediate supervisor immediately.

RUBBER GLOVE AND EYE PROTECTION POLICY

Because of the Occupational Safety Health Administration (OSHA) and the Mine Safety Health Administration (MSHA) standards, and **Your Company Name's** commitment to a safe work place for all employees, all personnel using cleaning chemicals on **Your Company Name** jobs will be required to wear rubber gloves and protective eye wear (provided by **Your Company Name**) when cleaning restrooms, shower rooms, or any other defined area.

This Policy is being enforced for these reasons:

1. To follow OSHA and MSHA Rules and Regulations.

2. To protect the employee from disease that may be transmitted in restroom cleaning.

3. To protect the employee from any injury to eyes when using cleaning chemicals.

If an employee refuses to wear rubber gloves or protective eye wear, **Your Company Name** will not be responsible for repercussions concerning the contraction of any disease or side effects from a reaction to the chemicals, or repercussions concerning eye injury from chemicals. Also, the company will NOT be responsible for medical bills incurred for failure to follow this policy.

SAFETY POLICY

At ***Your Company Name***, employee safety is everyone's business. Safety is to be given primary importance in every aspect of planning and performing all ***Your Company Name*** activities. Employees and management have shared responsibility in maintaining the workplace that is safe and injury free. ***Your Company Name*** wants to protect employees against industrial injury and illness, as well as minimize the potential loss of production. The employee's responsibility is to follow and observe all safety rules and procedures.

Please report all injuries (no matter how slight) to your manager and/or supervisor immediately, as well as anything that needs repair or is a safety hazard. If an accident does occur, you will be required to report the accident to your supervisor by the end of your shift and contact your District office within 24 hours of the injury. You will be asked to complete an accident review form. Below are some general safety rules. Your manager and/or supervisor may post other safety procedures in your work area.

- Read product labels before use. Never mix two chemicals together unless instructed on the label.
- Never use an unlabeled container.
- Avoid overloading electrical outlets with too many appliances or machines.
- Use flammable items, such as cleaning fluids, with caution.
- Walk --- don't run.
- Use stairs one at a time.
- Report to your manager and/or supervisor if you or a co-worker becomes ill or is injured.
- Ask for assistance when lifting heavy objects or moving heavy furniture.
- Smoke only in designated smoking areas.
- Never empty an ashtray into a wastebasket or any flammable receptacle.
- Wear or use appropriate safety equipment as required in

your work.
- Avoid "horseplay" or practical jokes.
- Start work on any machine only after safety procedures and requirements have been explained (and you understand them).
- Wear appropriate personal protective equipment, like shoes, hats, gloves, goggles, hearing protectors, etc. in designated areas or when working on an operation which requires their use.
- Keep your work area clean and orderly, and the aisles clear.
- Stack materials only to safe heights.
- Watch out for the safety of fellow employees.
- Use the right tool for the job, and use it correctly.
- Wear gloves whenever handling barrels, etc.
- Follow the blood borne pathogens exposure control plan/ policy.
- Loose clothing, jewelry or rings must be removed before operating machinery.

Remember that failure to adhere to these rules will be considered serious infractions of safety rules and will result in disciplinary action to the employee.

The employee will be required to purchase replacement of mandatory personal protective equipment that has been purposely destroyed or lost at cost. You may purchase personal protective equipment that is not mandatory.

Your Company Name will continue to provide a clean, safe and healthy place to work and will provide the best equipment possible. The employee is expected to work safely and observe all safety rules and to keep the premises clean and neat. Remember that carelessly endangering yourself or any employee may lead to disciplinary action, including possible termination.

VEHICLE POLICY & GUIDELINES

Each employee driving or riding in Company vehicles will wear seat belts at all time while vehicle is being driven. Smoking, eating, or drinking in vehicle will not be permitted. The vehicle will be kept neat, clean, and in an orderly manner during and after each shift.

DRUG AWARENESS PROGRAM

Following is the Drug-Free Workplace Policy for *Your Company Name*:

The unlawful manufacture, use, possession, distribution, sale or purchase of an illegal controlled substance while on Company premises or while conducting Company business is prohibited by law, and Company policy. Employees violating this policy will be subject to disciplinary action, up to and including immediate discharge.

As a condition of employment, it is required that employees abide by this policy and also notify the Company of any criminal drug stature conviction occurring in the workplace no later than five days after such conviction. The Company may, upon such notice, take appropriate personnel action up to and including termination.

The Company will exercise all appropriate steps to ensure compliance with this policy, including testing of applicants and employees.

Substance abuse is the harmful or dangerous use of alcohol or other illegal drugs or controlled substances. Anyone can have a problem with substance abuse. Everyone pays for substance abuse, and for this Company, it can affect employee safety, attendance, production, attitude, reliability, and much more. Our employees should have the opportunity to work in an environment free from the effect of alcohol and drugs.

Your Company Name recognizes that substance abuse is a problem which can be treated, but recognition of the problem is necessary for rehabilitation.

Agencies available to employees for help in drug related problems include Alcoholics Anonymous, Narcotics Anonymous, Cocaine Anonymous, National Institute on Drug Abuse Hotline (1-800-662-HELP), and area hospitals, health centers, and social services.

Drug awareness is a responsibility everyone must recognize. Inquiries about our drug-free workplace policy and program or agencies available for problem resolution may be made to the district office in your area. All employees have a legal and social obligation to be aware of the dangers of drugs, and to prevent the dangers of substance abuse in the workplace.

SUBSTANCE ABUSE POLICIES AND PROCEDURES

Your Company Name has a vital interest in providing and maintaining a healthy and safe working environment for its employees. The use of drugs and/or alcohol presents serious safety and health risks. The Company believes a drug free workplace will reduce workers' compensation injuries and promote the health and safety of our employees. It is with the desire of a drug-free workplace that the Company adopts the following policies and procedures:

1. ***Illegal or Controlled Substances.*** The unlawful manufacture, use, possession, distribution, sale or purchase of illegal or controlled substances* by an employee while on Company premises or while conducting Company business is prohibited. Having detectable amounts of illegal or controlled substances in your system while on duty on Company premises or in any Company vehicle, or while engaged in Company business, is also prohibited.

    Whenever illegal or controlled substances are detected through blood or urine analysis or other procedures, or it becomes otherwise known that an employee has in possession or is unlawfully manufacturing, using, distributing, selling, or purchasing illegal or controlled substances on or off Company premises, the employee will be subject to disciplinary action up to and including discharge.

Definitions:

* illegal or controlled substances means any drug:

    A. which is not legally obtainable; or

    B. which is legally obtainable but has not been legally obtained.

2. ***Alcohol.*** The unauthorized use, possession, distribution, or purchase of alcohol by an employee or being under the influence of alcohol while on Company premises or in any Company vehicle, or while conducting Company business, is prohibited. An employee who violates this prohibition will be subject to disciplinary action up to and including discharge.

3. ***Tests.*** As a condition of employment, the Company maintains the right to require employees to provide urine and blood samples for chemical tests/analysis and to submit to breath analysis or other tests as the Company deems necessary.

All tests will be confirmed by a certified laboratory. Test results may be used by the Company in legal proceedings involving the applicant or employee, including but not limited to workers' compensation and unemployment compensation proceedings. Employees have the right to refuse to cooperate in the required tests. Refusal to cooperate in such tests by any employee will be cause for disciplinary action up to and including discharge.

4. ***Disciplinary Action.*** An employee that tests positive for an illegal or controlled substance or alcohol will be terminated.

5. ***Types of Testing.*** To pursue the above policy, the Company requires the following testing:

    A. ***Applicant Testing.*** Applicants for employment who have successfully completed the initial screening process and who are applying for; (1) safety sensitive positions, including but not limited to vehicle operators, floor equipment operators, positions requiring the use of ladders, and positions involving trash removal, and (2) administrative and management positions, will be required to consent to and participate in a Substance Abuse Screen (drug test). The results of the Substance Abuse Screen will be evaluated when determining employment. Failure to pass the screen or failure to submit to the screen in a timely manner will result in a denial of employment.

    B. ***Employee Testing.***

        1. ***Post Accident Testing.*** Any employee engaged in Company activities who has an occupational accident, is a participant in an occupational accident, or sustains or causes an occupational injury which requires medical treatment by a physician, will submit to a Substance Abuse Screen. Failure to pass the Substance Abuse Screen or failure to submit to the screen in a timely manner (3 hours post injury or accident), will result in immediate disciplinary action up to and including discharge.

        2. ***"For Cause" Testing.*** A Substance Abuse Screen will be required when there is cause for the Company to believe, in the Company's discretion, that the employee has violated the policy concerning the use of controlled substances or alcohol. Failure to submit to or pass the drug screen will result in disciplinary action up to and including discharge.

3. ***Prescription Drugs.*** Any employee taking a controlled substance under a physician's order is encouraged to report use of the controlled substance to the designated Company official.

   The Substance Abuse Screen may include but is not limited to:

   * Amphetamines   * Benzodiazepines
   * Cocaine   * Barbiturates
   * Phencyclidine (PCP)   * Opiates
   * Methaqualone   * Alcohol
   * Marijuana

6. ***Reporting.*** It is required that employees abide by this policy and notify the Company of any criminal drug statute conviction for a violation occurring in the workplace no later than five (5) days after such conviction. The Company shall, upon such notice, take appropriate action up to termination.

   The employee understands that they may be required to submit to a urinalysis and/or blood testing as outlined in the Company policy, and that all test results become and remain the sole property of ***Your Company Name.*** Preplacement test results are not released to the applicant.

Richard D. Ollek, CBSE

THESE EMPLOYMENT POLICIES AND PROCEDURES DO NOT CREATE A CONTRACT. ALL EMPLOYEES OF THIS COMPANY ARE EMPLOYEES "AT WILL" AND CAN BE TERMINATED AT ANY TIME WITH OR WITHOUT CAUSE AT THE COMPANY'S DISCRETION. THESE EMPLOYMENT POLICIES AND PROCEDURES SERVE AS A GUIDE TO PERSONNEL. *YOUR COMPANY NAME* RESERVES THE RIGHT TO CHANGE THESE, OR ANY OTHER POLICIES, AT ANY TIME, FOR ANY REASON, WITH OR WITHOUT NOTICE. *YOUR COMPANY NAME* ALSO RESERVES THE RIGHT TO MAKE FINAL DECISIONS CONCERNING THE INTERPRETATION AND REVISION OF POLICIES AND PROCEDURES.

NO ONE WILL BE DENIED OPPORTUNITIES OR BENEFITS ON THE BASIS OF AGE, SEX, COLOR, RACE, CREED, NATIONAL ORIGIN, RELIGIOUS PERSUASION, MARITAL STATUS, POLITICAL BELIEF, OR DISABILITY THAT DOES NOT PROHIBIT PERFORMANCE OF ESSENTIAL JOB FUNCTIONS; NOR WILL ANYONE RECEIVE SPECIAL TREATMENT FOR THOSE REASONS.

You have joined an organization that is totally committed to provide the best service to "OUR" customer with the best-qualified personnel.

JOB AND PERFORMANCE DESCRIPTIONS

LIGHT DUTY SPECIALIST, VACUUM SPECIALIST, RESTROOM SPECIALIST, UTILITY SPECIALIST, FLOOR MACHINE SPECIALIST

All cleaning specialist jobs require the following qualifications

SPECIFIED RESPONSIBILITIES:

1. Perform cleaning duties at a maximum quality level.

2. Perform work within production time budgets and supply budgets.

3. Keep equipment clean and in good operating condition.

4. Follow all safety rules and participate in company's safety program.

5. Project a professional image and maintain good customer and public relations.

6. Adhere to company rules, policies, and operating procedures.

7. Reports to the site supervisor any equipment breakdowns, unsafe conditions, customer complaints and any other problems that may occur.

8. Adhere to tardiness and absenteeism policy.

9. Be able to work schedule as assigned by supervisor at various locations.

JOB AND PERFORMANCE DESCRIPTIONS

LIGHT DUTY SPECIALIST, VACUUM SPECIALIST, RESTROOM SPECIALIST, UTILITY SPECIALIST, FLOOR MACHINE SPECIALIST

All cleaning specialist jobs require the following qualifications

QUALIFICATION REQUIREMENTS:

To perform this successfully, an individual must be able to perform each essential duty satisfactorily. The requirements listed below are representative of the knowledge, skill and/or ability required. Reasonable accommodations may be made to enable individuals with disabilities to perform the essential functions.

Must have dependable transportation or be able to get to the job site scheduled.

LANGUAGE SKILLS:

Ability to read a limited number of two and three syllable words and to recognize similarities and differences between words and between series of numbers. Ability to print and speak simple sentences in English.

REASONING ABILITY:

Ability to apply common-sense understanding to carry out simple one- or two-step instructions. Ability to deal with standardized situations with only occasional or no variables.

JOB AND PERFORMANCE DESCRIPTIONS

LIGHT DUTY SPECIALIST, VACUUM SPECIALIST, RESTROOM SPECIALIST, UTILITY SPECIALIST, FLOOR MACHINE SPECIALIST

All cleaning specialist jobs require the following qualifications

PHYSICAL DEMANDS:

The physical demands described here are representative of those which must be met by an employee to successfully perform the essential functions of the job.

Must be able to perform manual tasks requiring strength and to be in good physical health.

While performing the duties of the job, the employee is regularly required to reach with hands and arms. The employee continually is required to stand, walk, stoop, kneel, crouch and bend. The employee is repetitively required to use hands and fingers, to handle objects and equipment, to push and pull, to climb and balance, and to talk and hear. The employee must repeatedly lift and/or move up to 50 pounds. Specific vision abilities required by this job include close vision, distance vision, color vision, peripheral vision, depth perception, and the ability to adjust focus.

WORK ENVIRONMENT:

The work environment characteristics described here are representative of that an employee encounters while performing the essential functions of this job. Reasonable accommodations may be made to enable individuals with disabilities to perform the essential functions. While performing the duties of this job, the employees occasionally work near moving mechanical parts and are occasionally exposed to toxic or caustic chemicals, risk of electric shock, and vibration. The noise level in the work environment is usually moderate.

While this job description is intended to be an accurate reflection of the job requirements, management reserves the right to modify, add or remove duties from particular jobs and to assign other duties as necessary.

POST-HIRE ASSIGNMENT FORM

District: _____ **Employee #** _____ **S.S. #** _____

First Name _____ **Middle** _____ **Last Name** _____

Address _____ **City** _____ **State** _____

Zip Code _____ **Day Phone** ( ) _____ **Night Phone** ( ) _____

Birth Date _____ **Male** _____ **Female** _____ **National Origin:** Caucasian _____

Black _____ Hispanic _____ Asian/Pacific Island _____ American Indian _____ Other _____

Hire Date _____ **Classification:** Cleaner P/T _____ Cleaner F/T _____

Site Acct. Rep. P/T _____ Site Acct. Rep. F/T _____ Area Acct. Rep. _____ Project Supv. _____

Asst. Project Mgr. _____ Project Mgr. _____ Operations Mgr. _____ Administrative Asst. _____

Clerical _____ Admin. Staff _____ **Job #** _____ **Job Name** _____

Address _____ City _____ State _____

Mail Check _____ **Pick Up Check** _____ **Pay Type:** Hourly _____ Salary _____ **Pay Rate** _____

Shift: _____ AM/PM to _____ AM/PM **Days:** ☐ Sun ☐ Mon ☐ Tue ☐ Wed ☐ Thur ☐ Fri ☐ Sat

Site Acct. Rep. _____ Pager ( ) _____ Phone ( ) _____

Area Acct. Rep. _____ Pager ( ) _____ Phone ( ) _____

Manager _____ Pager ( ) _____ Phone ( ) _____

Local Office Phone ( ) _____ Corporate Office, (000) 000-0000 or (800) 000-0000

In case of emergency, contact: Name _____ Phone ( ) _____

Address _____ City _____ State _____ Zip _____

Are there any emergency instructions, circumstances, medical needs, allergic responses or procedures **Your Company Name** should know? _____

At the time of my orientation for employment, I received instructions covering proper cleaning, safety rules and Company policies and have signed the Receipt & Acknowledgment Form.

Employee's Signature _____ **Date** _____

Management's Signature _____ **Date** _____

Deliver or FAX this form along with completed W-4 (Employee's allowance certificate), the I-9 (Employment Eligibility Verification) and the signed Receipt & Acknowledgment Form (*Your Company Name* Form ____) to the Corporate Office (FAX (000) 000-0000) prior to employee starting work.

Purpose of this form is to allow our new employee to begin work immediately and allow timekeeping functions to be performed. This will insure correct payroll checks without the need for changes or delays.

NOTE: This is not a substitute for the Pre- or Post-Hire employment application. Completed packets are to be retained in the District Offices.

YOUR COMPANY NAME Form _____
Revised Effective _____

Richard D. Ollek, CBSE

Employee Confidentially and Non-Compete Agreement

This Employee Confidentiality and Non-Compete Agreement ("Agreement") is made this ____day of _____, 20_____.

BY AND BETWEEN | *YOUR COMPANY NAME*
a (your state) corporation
hereinafter referred to as

"Employer"

AND

_____

,
an individual,
hereinafter referred to as

"Employee"

Employee desires to give, and Employer desires to receive from Employee, a covenant not to engage, either directly or indirectly, in competition with, or to solicit any customer, client, account, or employees of Employer and to not disclose confidential information.

Employer and Employee desire to set forth in writing the terms and conditions of their agreements and understandings.

NOW, THEREFORE, in consideration of the foregoing, of the mutual promises herein contained, and of other good and valuable consideration, the receipt and sufficiency of which are hereby acknowledged, the parties hereto, intending legally to be bound, hereby agree as follows:

SECTIONS:

1. <u>**Covenants Against Competition.**</u>

Employee acknowledges that the services to be rendered to Employer have a significant and material value to Employer, the loss of which cannot adequately be compensated by damages alone. In view of the significant and material value to Employer of the services of Employee for which Employer has employed Employee; and the confidential information obtained by or disclosed to Employee as an employee of Employer; and as a material inducement to Employer to employ Employee and to pay to Employee compensation for such services to be rendered for Employer by Employee (it being understood and agreed by the parties hereto that such non-compensation shall also be paid for and received in consideration hereof), Employee covenants and agrees as follows:

A. During Employee's employment by Employer and for a period of twenty-four (24) months after Employee ceases to be employed by Employer, Employee shall not directly or indirectly, either for Employee's own account or for the account of another, solicit or attempt to solicit customers of the Employer for the sale of the same or similar products or services sold to the customer of Employer. This prohibition shall apply to all customers or Employer purchasing services or products from Employer within twenty-four (24) months preceding the termination of Employee's employment with Employer.

B. During employment and for a period of twenty-four (24) months thereafter, Employee shall not, directly or indirectly, solicit for employment or employ any employee of Employer.

C. During employment, and thereafter for twenty-four (24) months, Employee shall not disclose to anyone any Confidential Information. For the purposes of this Agreement, "Confidential Information" shall include any of Employer's confidential, proprietary or trade secret information that is disclosed to Employee or Employee otherwise learns in the course of employment such as, but not limited to, business plans, customer lists, employee lists, pricing lists, financial statements, software diagrams, flow charts and product plans.

2. At Will.

Employee acknowledges that Employee's employment is at will. Employer or Employee may terminate employment at any time, with or without notice, for any reason or no reason whatsoever. Nothing in this Agreement shall constitute a promise of employment, or promise to employment for any particular duration or rate of pay.

3. Accounting for Profits.

Employee covenants and agrees that, if Employee shall violate any covenants or agreements in Section 1 hereof, Employer shall be entitled to an accounting and repayment of all profits, compensation, commissions, remuneration's or benefits which Employee directly or indirectly has realized and/or may realize as a result of, growing out of or in connection with any such violation; such remedy shall be in addition to and not in limitation of any injunctive relief or other rights or remedies to which Employer is or may be entitled at law or in equity or under this Agreement.

4. Reasonableness of Restrictions.

A. Employee has carefully read and considered the provisions of Section 1 hereof and, having done so, agrees that the restrictions set forth therein (including, but not limited to, the time period of restriction and the geographical areas of restriction) are fair and reasonable and are reasonably required for the protection of the interests of Employer, its officers, directors, shareholders and other employees.

B. In the event that, notwithstanding the foregoing, any part of the covenants set forth in Section 1 hereof shall be held to be invalid or unenforceable, the remaining parts thereof shall nevertheless continue to be valid and enforceable as though the invalid or unenforceable parts had not been included therein. In the event that any provision of Section 1 relating to time period and/or areas of restriction shall be declared by a court of competent jurisdiction to exceed the maximum time period or areas such court deems reasonable and enforceable, the agreed upon time period and/or areas of restriction shall be deemed to become and thereafter be the maximum time period and/or areas which such court deems reasonable and enforceable.

5. <u>Burden and Benefit</u>.

This Agreement shall be binding upon, and shall inure to the benefit of, Employer and Employee, and their respective heirs, personal and legal representatives, successors and assigns.

6. <u>Governing Law</u>.

Construction and interpretation of this Agreement shall at all times and in all respects be governed by the laws of the State of _____.

7. <u>Severability</u>.

The provisions of this Agreement (including particularly, but not limited to, the provisions of Section 1 hereof) shall be deemed severable, and the invalidity or unenforceability of any one or more of the provisions hereof shall not affect the validity and enforceability of the other provisions hereof.

8. <u>Employer</u>.

As used herein, the term "Employer" shall include any corporation which is at any time a parent or subsidiary of Employer.

9. Notices.

Any notice required to be or otherwise given hereunder shall be sufficient if in writing, and sent by certified or registered mail, return receipt requested, first-class postage prepaid, as follows:

If to Employer: *Your Company Name*

Your Company Address

Your Company City, State, Zip

If to Employee: **Name** _____

Address _____

City, State, Zip _____

or to such other address designated by either party following notice to the other.

10. Entire Agreement.

This Agreement contains the entire agreement and understanding by and between Employer and Employee with respect to the covenant against competition herein referred to, and no representations, promises, agreements or understandings, written or oral, not herein contained shall be of any force or effect. No change or modification hereof shall be valid or binding unless the same is in writing and signed by the party intended to be bound.

11. No Waiver.

No waiver of any provision of this Agreement shall be valid unless the same is in writing and signed by the party against whom such waiver is sought to be enforced; moreover, no valid waiver of any provision of this Agreement at any time shall be deemed a waiver of any other provision of this Agreement at such time or will be deemed a valid waiver of such provision at any other time.

12. Headings.

The headings used herein are for the convenience of the parties only and shall not be used to define, enlarge or limit any term of this Agreement.

IN WITNESS WHEREOF, Employer and Employee have duly executed this Agreement under seal as of the day and year first above written.

<table>
<tr><td align="center">EMPLOYER</td><td align="center">EMPLOYEE</td></tr>
<tr><td align="center">Your Company Name</td><td></td></tr>
<tr><td>By _____</td><td>By _____</td></tr>
<tr><td align="center">(print)</td><td align="center">(print)</td></tr>
<tr><td>_____</td><td>_____</td></tr>
<tr><td align="center">(signature)</td><td align="center">(signature)</td></tr>
<tr><td>_____</td><td>_____</td></tr>
<tr><td align="center">DATE</td><td align="center">DATE</td></tr>
</table>

Receipt & Acknowledgment
of *Your Company Name*
Employment Policies and Procedures Hand Book

A copy of our Employment Policies and Procedures Handbook is being given to you. This is an important document intended to help you become acquainted with *Your Company Name*. This document will serve as a guide; but it is not the final word in all cases. Individual circumstances may call for individual attention.

Because the general business atmosphere of *Your Company Name* and economic conditions are ever changing, the contents of this Handbook may be changed at any time at the discretion of *Your Company Name*. No changes in any benefit, policy or rule will be made without due consideration of the mutual advantages, disadvantages, benefits and responsibilities such changes will have on you as an employee and on *Your Company Name*.

Please read the following statements and sign below to indicate your receipt and acknowledgment of the *Your Company Name* Employment Policies and Procedures Handbook.

* I have received and read, or have had read to me, a copy of the *Your Company Name* Employment Policies and Procedures Handbook. I understand that the policies, rules and benefits described in it is subject to change at the sole discretion of *Your Company Name* at any time. I understand that this document replaces (supersedes) all other previous Employment Policies and Procedures for *Your Company Name* as of August 1, 1998.
  □ I received a copy and will comply / **initial** _____

* I further understand that my employment can be terminated at will, either by myself or *Your Company Name* regardless of the length of my employment or the granting of benefits of any kind.
  □ I understand and will comply / **initial** _____

* I understand that no contract of employment other than "at will" has been expressed or implied, and that no circumstances arising out of my employment will alter my "at will" employment relationship unless expressed in writing, with the understanding specifically set forth and signed by myself and the President of *Your Company Name*
  □ I understand / **initial** _____

* I understand that I may be required to submit to urinalysis and/or blood testing as outlined in the Company Policy, and that all test results become and remain the sole property of *Your Company Name* Replacement test results are not released to me. I have read the Company policies, procedures, and requirements of the Drug Awareness Program and understand them completely.
  □ I understand / **initial** _____

A copy of this form must be forwarded to the *Your Company Name*'s Corporate Office
YOUR COMPANY NAME Form ____
Revised Effective _____
Page 1 of 3

136

*   I understand that I will be required to surrender my picture identification badge upon termination of employment in order to receive my final paycheck. I will report my lost or stolen identification badge to my supervisor immediately and will pay the charge of $ 5.00 to have a new identification badge made.

☐ I understand / initial _____

*   I understand that <u>my signature below</u> indicates that **I have read, or have had read to me, and do understand** the above statements and have **received a copy** of the *Your Company Name* Employment Policies and Procedures Handbook. I have **received orientation and training** by a *Your Company Name* representative.

Safety and Individual Policies contained within the Employment Policies and Procedures Handbook which was given to me were (<u>answer the following questions</u>) (Please check the block you desire and initial):

Welcome Letter/You're Part of Our Team	**Uniform and Dress Code Policy**	**Rubber Glove and Eye Protection Policy**
☐ I received both letters	☐ I will comply	☐ I will comply
☐ I did not receive both letters	☐ I am Refusing to comply	☐ I am Refusing to comply
Initial _____	Initial _____	Initial _____
Hazard Communication Training & Acknowledgment	**Safety Policy**	**Sexual Harassment Policy**
☐ I was trained	☐ I will comply	☐ I will comply
☐ I was <u>not</u> trained	☐ I am Refusing to comply	☐ I am Refusing to comply
Initial _____	Initial _____	Initial _____
Group Insurance Acknowledgment	**Non-Disclosure of Confidential Information**	**Time & Attendance Policy**
☐ I want to enroll	☐ I will comply	☐ I will comply
☐ I am Refusing enrollment	☐ I am Refusing to comply	☐ I am Refusing to comply
Initial _____	Initial _____	Initial _____

_____   _____
Employee's Printed Name   Position

_____   _____
Employee's Signature   Initials   Date

_____   _____
Your Company Name Representative Printed Name   Position

_____   _____
Your Company Name Representative Signature   Date

A copy of this form must be forwarded to the *Your Company Name*'s Corporate Office

YOUR COMPANY NAME Form _____
Revised Effective _____
Page 2 of 3

Richard D. Ollek, CBSE

UNIFORM RECEIPT ACKNOWLEDGMENT FORM

All Employees

My signature below signifies that as a full- or part-time employee of **Your Company Name**, I have received:

ITEM	**COLOR**	**QUANTITY**
_____	_____	_____
_____	_____	_____
_____	_____	_____
_____	_____	_____

I also understand that upon termination of my employment, either by **Your Company Name** or by myself, I must return the items above within 72 hours of termination.

_____   _____
SIGNATURE   DATE

A copy of this form must be forwarded to the _Your Company Name_'s Corporate Office
YOUR COMPANY NAME Form _____
Revised Effective _____
Page 3 of 3

138

STEP 4

ORIENTATION

Includes:

Procedures for Orientation

1. May be done one-on-one, or in a class setting.

   - Should be completed prior to the employee going to the job site.

   - Should be conducted in English or other language versions.

2. Welcome each person to the class.

   - Use the "Welcome Letter" and "You're Part of Our Team" letter as a guide.

       o Give a brief history of *Your Company Name* and its locations with emphasis on your District.

       o Show the Organization Chart.

       o Stress *Your Company Name* goals and teamwork.

           * Reputation for quality service.

           * Pride in your work.

           * Treating people with respect and dignity.

           * Stress each employee is a Professional.

           * Stress each employee is responsible for their own actions and are held accountable.

           * Stress Good team attitude.

3. Show the Team Cleaning overview video to all employees.

Then their specific job. In each case, explain safety, MSDS and chemicals used.

- **Light Duty Specialist**

  o Show Light Duty Specialist video.

  o Show brute and proper lifting techniques.

  o Demonstrate glass cleaning techniques and chemicals.

  o Demonstrate carpet spotting and chemicals.

  o Advise that not all surfaces in the entire building are dusted each night, but on a rotation basis (Quad area cleaning).

- **Vacuum Specialist**

  o Show backpack video (English or other language version).

  o Demonstrate proper way to put on and wear the backpack.

  o Demonstrate how to protect the cord from stress.

  o Demonstrate vacuuming style.

  o Demonstrate how to check the bags, filters, and emptying and cleaning procedures.

  o Have the employee empty the bag, remove and replace the filters.

  o Have the employee put on the backpack and

adjust for proper fit and demonstrate vacuuming style.

o   Stress the importance of proper fit and safety.

o   Stress turning off lights and locking doors.

- **Restroom Specialist**

    o   Show the restroom cleaning video (English or other language version).

    o   Review procedures and show chemicals and tools.

        *   Stress eye protection and rubber gloves.

        *   Show chemicals used.

        *   Fill dispensers first (demonstrate).

        *   Show sweeping techniques.

        *   Clean fixtures and glass.

        *   Show toothbrush and use.

        *   Show wall, partition and door cleaning techniques.

        *   Mopping techniques.

- **Utility Specialist**

    o   Show backpack video (English or other language version).

* Demonstrate lifting techniques for trash removal.

* Demonstrate chemicals for the use of glass and metal cleaners.

* Demonstrate Vacuum Specialist duties as this is the preferred method of sweeping certain hard surface floors.

* Demonstrate dust and wet mopping and chemicals used.

* Review staircase cleaning.

* Demonstrate use of buffing machine if the job assigned requires the use.

o Review procedures and show chemicals and tools.

- Floor Machine Specialist

    o Show appropriate videos (English or other language version).

    * Buffing.

    * Stripping and recoating.

    * Carpet cleaning.

    o Show the equipment to be used.

    o Review chemicals and the process for application.

4. Quick overview of Employee Handbook.

- Attendance and punctuality (attendance bonus).

    o Proper timekeeping procedures.

        * Clocking in on electronic timekeeping system.

        * Clocking out on electronic timekeeping system.

    o If you're sick, call in 5 hours prior to start of your shift.

- Review the pay periods and paydays.

- Emphasize wearing of uniform and badges on each shift.

    o Issue uniforms.

    o Issue ID badges.

- Breakage policy:

    o Importance of being careful to protect property.

    o Do not take anything on or in desks or elsewhere.

    o Report all breakage.

- Explain the benefits:

    o Vacation and holiday policy.

    o Group Insurance (over 30 hours/week).

- Sexual Harassment will not be tolerated:

  o We have an anonymous hot line 1-800-XXX-XXXX Ext. XXX.

  o Use hot line for any reason.

  o Drug and Alcohol Awareness (Drug Free Workplace).

    * Applicant testing.

    * For-cause testing.

    * Post-accident testing.

  o Explain rules of conduct.

  o Review vehicle policy & guidelines.

- Review Safety.

  o Stress the importance of safety:

    * Lifting

      • If something is too heavy, don't attempt to lift or move it without help.

      • Lifting belts.

    * Slips and Falls.

      • Use safety signs when working on wet floors.

      • Wear rubber sole shoes (unless your job site requires different foot wear).

   * Use of rubber gloves and eye protection.

      • Mandatory in restrooms.

      • Selected job sites may vary.

   * Hazard communication program (MSDS).

      • Location in building.

      • Necessity of labeling bottles (each bottle must have a label).

5. Questions and Answers.

   • Final welcome to the TEAM.

   • Company news is distributed in newsletter.

     o Input for newsletter is encouraged.

     o All training classes are announced monthly. Plan to attend class that enhances your professionalism.

   • Encourage suggestions for improvement of any process.

New-Hire Processing Checklist

I.   Pre-employment job application

II.   Orientation

     A.   Explain pay day calendar - we get paid twice a month, not every 2 weeks.

     B.   Emphasize the following in the Employee Policy Manual:

         1.   Attendance and punctuality

            a.   Must call in 5 hours prior to shift if not going to work.

            b.   Must call if going to be late.

         2.   Hours and Location - advise that hours and location of job may change.

         3.   Training - advise that employees may be re-trained for other jobs.

         4.   Uniforms - advise uniform and ID badge must be worn at all times.

         5.   Employee conduct

            a.   Point out that rules in the first section when broken result in written or oral discipline.

            b.   Point out that rules in the second section when broken result in immediate termination.

         6.   Resignations - advise that we require at least two weeks notice when possible.

         7.   Appeals - advise that if supervisor terminates them, and they feel the cause is unjust, they should appeal to the Area Supervisor. Then the Production Supervisor, and finally the District Manager.

         8.   Attendance bonus - advise that we do not have sick pay, but well pay. If employee completes 90 days without missing, receives a free shift.

         9.   Vacation - advise full-time employees receive vacation pay.

         10.   Breaks - advise employees working 6 hours or more, receive 30 minute break.

         11.   Group insurance - advise full-time employees are eligible for group insurance after 90 days. Company pays for 50% of the employees monthly premium.

         12.   Holiday Pay – advise full-time employees are paid for listed holidays.

     C.   Employee Work Ethic and Safety Policy Packet

         1.   Advise them of "Welcome to the Company" letter.

         2.   Advise them of *Your Company Name* Team Work letter.

         3.   Advise them of Rubber Glove and Eye Protection Policy.

         4.   Advise them of Hazard Communication Training.

         5.   Advise them of Lifting Belt Policy.

         6.   Advise them of Sexual Harassment Policy & anonymous 800 number.

     D.   Have employee read and verify that all blanks are filled and that signature of employee and *Your Company Name* Representative/Trainer is complete.

     E.   Receipt and Acknowledgment Form - have employee complete and verify that all blanks are filled with appropriate checks, initials and signatures.

     F.   Medical Review - have employee complete and verify that all blanks are filled with appropriate checks, initials and signatures.

     G.   W4 - have employee complete and verify that # of exemptions are documented with signature and date.

     H.   I9 - have employee complete top portion, then we fill out bottom with identification they provide according to I9 requirements.

New-Hire Processing Checklist

I. Uniform - provide employee with work shirt or smock. Full-time = 2;
    Part-time = 1.

J. Badge - provide employee with badge.

K. Uniform Receipt Acknowledgment Form - have employee complete.

L. Post-Hire Assignment Form-we complete, then have employee sign & date.

M. Copies - make copies of:
    1. Identification provided by employee (Soc. Sec. Card, Green Card, Driver's License.)
    2. Post-Hire Assignment Form - give copy to employee, we keep original.
    3. Uniform Receipt Acknowledgment Form - give copy to employee, we keep original.

N. Be sure employee knows when, where & to whom they are to report for work. Write this on their copy of the Post-Hire Assignment Form.

III. When all is completed:

A. Employee should leave with:
    1. Employee Policy Manual
    2. Pay Day Calendar
    3. Copy of Post-Hire Assignment Form
    4. Copy of Electronic Timekeeping Procedures Form
    5. Copy of Employee Confidentiality and Non-Compete Agreement
    6. Copy of Uniform and Badge Receipt Acknowledgment Form
    7. Uniform shirt or smock
    8. ID badge

B. We should have for personnel file:
    1. Pre-employment job application
    2. Post-Hire Assignment Form
    3. W4
    4. I9
    5. Electronic Timekeeping Procedures Form
    6. Employee Confidentiality and Non-Compete Agreement
    7. Company Policies Receipt and Acknowledgment Form
    8. Copy of Identification - Soc. Sec. Card, Green Card, Driver's License
    9. Uniform and Badge Receipt Acknowledgment Form
    10. Completed medical insurance forms (either acceptance or denial)
    11. New-Hire Processing Checklist (this document)

IV. Final Steps:

A. Copies - make copies and distribute to payroll:
    1. Post-Hire Assignment Form
    2. W4
    3. I9
    4. Electronic Timekeeping Procedures Form
    5. Receipt and Acknowledgment Form
    6. Completed medical insurance forms (either acceptance or denial)

B. Files - make label for personnel file for each new employee and file appropriately.

Completed by: _____ Date: _____

At the end of this information packet is what I always felt was one of the more important documents I had. It is a New-Hire Processing Checklist. By using this as a guideline we were able to follow up and assure that we had all of the information we needed for the proper processing of the our new GREAT employee. I strongly suggest you create something similar if you have not already done so. (Whatever happened to the old handshake and let's go to work procedure? Progress I guess).

The title of this book is "Finding, Training, and Keeping GREAT Service Employees 101" and I submit to you that having a systematic procedure for assimilating new employees into your company is one of the key elements in the TRAINING AND KEEPING process. Use this hiring process manual as a guide wherever it can be helpful. It may just save you thousands of hours and dollars you would have to spend starting from scratch. If you already have a hiring process manual, review this one and adapt it wherever it will help you.

In addition, the manual includes a sample employee policy manual. Again, compare it to what you have, use whatever you can to make yours better. If yours is better than the one shown, I congratulate you and encourage you to keep on improving your organization.

The hiring process manual information, as well as the job descriptions shown in Chapter 17 are also available on CD via our web site, www. consultantsincleaning.com.

Thought for the day: **Want a new method of terminating someone? Take them to lunch and buy theirs to go.**

- Ollekism

CHAPTER 12

THE IMPORTANCE OF TRAINING

You will recall in chapter 10 we listed the top reasons employees leave our service companies. You may also remember that 2 of the top reasons were connected to not being told what to do and if they were told what to do, they weren't trained on how to do it.

In the service industry today, no subject receives more discussion and less results than does training. Nearly every proposal that I have seen in the contract cleaning and related services industry will have a section on how they employ trained personnel. And you know what, most companies do have trained personnel---POORLY TRAINED, that is.

When I conduct workshops on this subject of training, one of the exercises we have the participants do in groups is to list what better training of the worker means to them and their company.

Let's list here some of the ones that come to mind:

◊ REDUCES TURNOVER—At the rate of $500 plus per employee to put someone on the payroll, it doesn't take a genius to determine that this benefit comes near the top of the list. Again, I suggest you review the number of W-2's your company provided for everyone that worked for you last year, determine the excess over your normal payroll and you'll see the dollars you wasted. You may want to get some nausea relief pills before you do this exercise. I know I needed them the first time I saw the number.

◊   HELPS RETAIN CUSTOMERS---Ever had a customer tell you when they canceled that the main reason was your high turnover? Most service companies, if honest, will admit they have, at least once, been told that. So, factor in the sales cost you have in finding new prospects and turning them into long term customers and you have another big number and big reason to provide a quality training program in your company.

◊   HELPS OBTAIN NEW CUSTOMERS---One of the questions being asked often today by prospective customers either during the early sales process or the sales presentation process is, "What's your turnover rate"? I have seen service contractors eliminated through this process. I have also seen service contractors become extremely creative in how they determine their turnover rate when they have to answer this question. I didn't know there were so many different ways to determine turnover rates until I heard some contractors trying to explain their number to a prospective customer.

◊   CREATES A SAFER WORK ENVIRONMENT---You may not have thought of this one but properly trained employees have fewer accidents and fewer accidents result in lower workers compensation premiums for the company. Here again, many prospective customers are asking the qualifying question of prospective service providers, "What is your workers compensation modification rate?" Many prospects today will not allow you to present a proposal if your modification rate is over 1.00. I am aware of a sizable Building Service Contractor who was the incumbent service provider who lost a major piece of business because their modification rate went to 1.01. The customer was so safety conscious they would not allow a waiver even though this BSC had been their provider for many years. The customer was that intent on a safe working environment. I know, you are saying there must have been another reason and they just used this as an excuse. I don't think so but even if they did, why give them the opportunity to use this excuse. Develop an ongoing training program and keep the premiums at a manageable level.

◊ LOWER LABOR COSTS---You, no doubt, have heard or said the phrase, "Why is their never enough time to do it right the first time, but always time to do it over?" Well, with the proper training, there are fewer times the job has to be done over. Make sense? Not to mention when a customer has to call you to complain that a job was not done correctly, you have lost some credibility with that customer which brings you one step closer to making them a "former customer".

◊ LOWER MATERIAL COSTS---This one goes hand in hand with the lowering of labor costs. If a worker is trained in the proper way of using materials needed in his or her job, it stands to reason that there is less waste and lower overall cost. 'Nuff said here.

◊ LESS EQUIPMENT REPAIR---I can recall, prior to having a systematic training program and an in house repair department, having telephone conversations with the company that repaired our equipment about the misuse our equipment was getting. There will always be those who misuse equipment no matter how much training you give them and those are the ones you want to take to lunch and buy theirs to go. But, most people WANT to use the equipment properly. Train them properly and your equipment repair costs WILL GO DOWN.

I remember at one of our quarterly supervisor's/management meetings, one of my key managers was explaining for the umpteenth time how to properly empty a vacuum bag. As he was going through the process, one of the participants asked, "Bill, how many times are we going to have to hear how to properly empty a vacuum bag?" "I will continue to repeat this process until we learn how to do it properly", was the reply. You see as fate would have it, Bill had taken the vacuum he was demonstrating the procedure with from the building where the questioning participant worked. We did not embarrass this person in front of his peers but did talk with him after the meeting that it was his vacuum we were using and that it would be best if he listened more and talked less and then followed the correct procedure.

I can go on with this exercise but I have probably hit on the major reasons for doing training that most impact the profitability of your company. Let me suggest that you conduct this exercise with your staff and see what the answers are and then build a training workshop around their answers and the ones you want to discuss that they may not have listed. Try it, you'll like it.

As a consultant, I am sometimes asked by clients to attend presentations they are receiving from Building Service Contractors. They are asking me to listen to the presentations with them and help determine if they should make a change and, if so, who might be the best choice. I always leave the choice with the client but do try to offer constructive points from the presentations.

As best I can remember, every presentation I have listened to had a portion devoted to the "trained personnel" of the aspiring service provider.

Inasmuch as training is almost an obsession with me, I would suggest to my client they ask these things from the presenters:

◊   We would like to have a checklist of your new employee orientation and training process.

◊   Please provide us a schedule of your upcoming training events.

◊   We would like to schedule a visit to tour your training facility and to meet your trainer(s).

Generally these are questions that provide some separation of the presenters. I listen carefully to the responses and then advise my clients as to which of the presenters MAY have stretched the 'trained personnel" concept just a bit. Nevertheless, I do encourage my client to follow through on the request. Sometimes they do, sometimes they don't.

How about your company? Do you provide genuine training or is yours a training program of "on the job" which means you really don't have a training program?

You may be asking yourself right now, "Self, why is Dick being so hard on everyone about training? Doesn't he understand that our people turnover fast, so what's the use, they'll be gone before I can complete any kind of thorough training"? Let me suggest that if every company had a detailed, professional training program for all levels of its company, the employees might stay longer. Remember 2 of the top 4 reasons why people leave?

Talking about turnover, I once visited with a restaurant mogul who had over 300 fast food locations and we were discussing the perils of turnover in the service business. As I was explaining my unacceptable 80% turnover rate at the time, he explained to me that his average line worker employee lasted on the job for 8 days---8 DAYS. Now that's turnover. I believe he needed a training program or at least a better one.

"AM I COMMUNICATING?"

One of the things that makes training more difficult in the real world today is the diverse cultures and different nationalities that we have in our GREAT employee workforce. In a recent workshop I was conducting, this subject was being discussed and I was explaining the process I had used for being able to train in English and Spanish. I was quite proud of myself until one of the workshop participants who was a Buildings and Grounds Superintendent at a large university explained to the group that he had to convert all of his training materials into 28 different languages so he could effectively communicate with his staff. Two didn't seem like such a big accomplishment after he was finished explaining his dilemma.

Then we need to add to the equation our new generation of people who are text messaging everything in a language that certainly looks foreign to me. I have learned that if I want to communicate with my grandchildren, I must learn this new language and I keep working on it. And I thought sign language was difficult.

But assuming for the moment that you are not conducting your training programs in text message language, here is an exercise you may want to conduct with your staff to see if you are even communicating at all. Ask everyone to give their one or two word definition of the following words:

- ☐ **Fire**
- ☐ **Diamond**
- ☐ **Train**
- ☐ **Hike**
- ☐ **Bad**

Have your participants write down the first words that come to their mind when they see these words. Now, you do the same. Then ask for the definitions and write them on a white board or large pad.

Let's see some of the answers you will probably get. What answers did you give?

- ☐ **Fire----Terminate, hot, flames, alarm, unemployment, emergency.**
- ☐ **Diamond---Expensive, ring, baseball, girlfriend, wife.**
- ☐ **Train---Locomotive, tracks, teach, learn.**
- ☐ **Hike---Mountain, take a hike, raise in pay.**
- ☐ **Bad---Good, cool, broke the rules, kewl.**

Take a close look at the definitions to these words and you can see why we sometimes (maybe all the time) have trouble communicating in today's world. Add to this the different languages we now encounter, along with the new text message language and you can better understand the desperate need for effective training in today's service world. I will go so far as to suggest that the success or failure of your individual service company will depend on the success or failure of the recruiting and training programs you implement in your company. A pretty bold statement but I believe it to be true.

In looking at the word "fire" I am reminded of the story a friend of mine told me recently about learning business vocabulary at an early age. He tells the story that as a young student he had a part time job sacking and carrying out groceries at the neighborhood store. One day as he was putting groceries in the trunk of a ladies car, a sack broke and he had groceries all over the ground. The lady immediately went inside and complained to the store manager which resulted in him being called to the office. After some discussion, the store manager told my friend he was going to terminate him. My friend responded back, "What's that mean"? The manager replied, "It means you're fired". "NOW I UNDERSTAND," my friend said. We need to be sure everyone understands what we are talking about.

Want to have some more fun with the exercise on definition of words? Ask your participants in small groups to create a sentence or two using the various definitions of the words they listed. It will become readily apparent how confusion can run rampant if not everyone is using the same basis for communication in your company.

"GENERATION MISCOMMUNICATON"

You no doubt have heard or read all about the different generations we now have in the work force. There are the traditionalists, the baby boomers, generation "X", generation "Y". Some call them generation why?

Communicating with all the different generations presents an entirely new set of communication problems. Let me give you some examples.

I come from the traditionalist group, that group born before 1946, commonly known as the group that came over in the covered wagon. When I speak of a record, I am thinking of my old 45 rpm by Fats

Domino or Little Richard. When speaking of a record today you wonder what crime was committed.

I recall watching a rerun recently of the "Law and Order" television series where the star Jerry Orbach, "Lenny", was interviewing a young security guard who had fallen asleep while on duty which allowed a murder to occur. Jerry asks the young man, "Who do you think you are, Rip VanWinkle"?, to which the young man replies, "Who"?. Rip Van Winkle was one of the main stories my generation grew up reading. We thought EVERYONE knew who Rip Van Winkle was.

In 2005 I was conducting a training class on safety in my own company. I was explaining the importance and necessity of wearing the proper foot wear while at work and told the group that wearing thongs was not permitted to which my young new recruits burst out laughing. You see, in my day, flip flops were called thongs and today a thong is…well, something entirely different.

Think about it. Those of us who are of the older generation actually had to manage a company without

- **High speed floor machines**
- **Backpack vacuums for everyday use**
- **Cell phones**
- **Computers**
- **The internet**
- **GPS units**
- **Bidding and estimating software**
- **PDA's**
- **PowerPoint sales presentations**
- **Computer spreadsheets to confuse us**

Okay, you traditionalists, start naming some other things you had to do without.

You of the younger generation are probably saying something like, "No wonder things were so screwed up before I got here".

Thought for the day: **There is no use doing well that which you should not be doing at all.**

-   Thomas Connellan

CHAPTER 13

SO HOW DO WE TRAIN?

After spending my entire adult life in the cleaning industry, training employees and visiting countless other companies who are trying to reduce their turnover and improve customer retention, I am convinced for many, it is not that they don't want to, it is that they don't understand the difference between training adults and training children. Oh yes, there are those who espouse the theory that why train, they will leave anyway. But I continue to believe that most organizations want to do the right thing.

It is my hope that those who have the "why train" thinking will buy this book, read it with a positive attitude, and take action to "do the right thing".

I have an Ollekism:

> *"It is better to train your employees and have them leave than to not train them and have them stay."*

Think about it. Wouldn't it be much easier on all of us if the world we work in and the career we have chosen was full of qualified, trained GREAT employees? So, if you train them well, chances are good they won't leave. But if they do, you have greatly improved the industry and who knows, they may come back to you once they find the competitor that offered them the moon doesn't really have anything to offer. So you are ahead either way.

So let's examine this whole idea of training adults vs. training children.

First off, I think you will agree that you can order or mandate your adult employees into a training class but you can't force them to learn. Agreed? The fact is adults learn differently than children do. I believe if you ask training professionals they will readily agree with me. While there are several theories about why adults learn differently than children, there are several things we know for sure. Adults have an entirely different motivation concerning learning and they filter information through a different mindset than do children.

I think it is important to have a basic understanding of how adults learn when you start to think and talk about improving your company's training process. Most people's experience with training is limited to what they were exposed to as children, sitting in a classroom listening to the teacher explain the topic of the day. But if you try to approach training that way in your organization, I submit to you that your training will fail. Bold words but I truly believe them.

"MOTIVATION TO LEARN"

So how can you motivate your potential GREAT employees to learn? Sometimes this can seem like an impossible task when you are trying to teach someone to clean a toilet. There are several important facts we need to know about motivation of adults:

☐ Adult learners can be motivated by appealing to their personal growth and wealth---in order to motivate adults to learn, you must tell them the "WIIFM"—What's in it for me?" They need to know the justification for taking the time and effort to learn something. Adults need to know why it is important to learn something. Why it is important for them. One of the most powerful motivators is appealing to personal growth or wealth. In the situation of a job, the prospect of earning a promotion to supervisor or manager is a fairly strong "What's in it for me"? For some, just the motivation of a regular paycheck that may have been missing for some time can be a strong motivating factor. This also goes a long way in addressing one of the main reasons potentially GREAT people leave our employ. Remember which one? Right, "There doesn't seem to be any room for advancement".

☐ Personal recognition can be a powerful motivator---it is a known fact and I pointed it out in the chapter on effective ads for recruiting, that many people suffer from low self- esteem. The prospect of learning a new skill can offer a boost to that low self esteem. The fact that you want to provide them with the skills can be appealing and a strong motivator.

"CHILDREN VS. ADULTS IN LEARNING"

I want to discuss here some of the differences in learning between children and adults. I think the differences are substantial and I also believe, as stated earlier in this chapter, it is imperative that you know the difference or your training will not succeed.

CHILDREN rely on others to decide what is important to learn. They go to school every day and the teacher has a lesson plan laid out for them that they are expected to learn and are tested on their comprehension of the material.

ADULTS, on the other hand, decide for themselves what is important to learn. For example, you probably decided to buy and read this book on your own. It is not part of a high school economics class required reading to pass the course. You may have been told, however, by a boss to read this book but you are in control of whether you read it or not. What's the worst that can happen? Don't answer that.

CHILDREN accept information being presented in the class at face value. If the teacher says there are 24 crayons in the carton, the child believes it because they trust what their teacher says is true.

ADULTS will do what? They will want to count the crayons in the carton because they remember years ago buying some and being shorted two crayons in the carton. Their experience has taught them to be cautious as to what people tell them. They have learned that people do not always tell the truth. They have listened to some of the members of congress.

CHILDREN are told and expect that what they are learning now to be useful to them in the long term. They are led to believe that the education they are getting now will result in a better paying job, etc. If college students didn't believe that, what would be their motivation for getting the education?

ADULTS, on the other hand, expect that what they are learning will be useful immediately. That is why many people attend conventions, seminars, workshops and the like. They expect to learn something that they can take back to their job or career and put to immediate use. It is my guess you did not read this book with the intention that in 5 or 10 years there might be something useful. You are reading it because you are hopeful of getting an idea or four that will help you NOW. (I hope so too.)

CHILDREN have little or no experience upon which to draw---they have relatively "clean slates". They still believe everything they are told (scary). Think back to your childhood. Your parents and teachers were your source for information and truth. As you grew older, questions started to arise, and by the time you were a teenager you had answers to questions that had not even been asked. (Just kidding?)

ADULTS, on the other hand have much past experience upon which to draw. They have had time to form their opinions and viewpoints which many times will differ dramatically from the very people they were relying on for information in their youth. I know many of my viewpoints have changed from when I was a child. I don't necessarily disagree with what I was told, I just have more facts now on which to form an opinion. It is important to remember that the employees you are wanting to train also have had the opportunity to learn new and different views on a variety of the subjects you may be trying to teach them.

Recognizing the differences will make a huge impact on whether your training is successful. I urge you to keep them embedded in your mind as you develop and execute a training plan.

I have had the opportunity to visit many companies and observe and advise them on establishing an ongoing training program. I can remember being asked to assist a company who called me in an almost panic state. They had a very sizable company, had developed an elaborate orientation and training program, but still were experiencing an annual turnover rate well in excess of 300%.

In order for me to be of assistance to them I had to first see what they were currently doing. They had an orientation class every night from 6 PM to 10 PM in their training center. They were turning over people so fast that they had the class five nights per week. One of the problems they were having is that people would attend the orientation class but then not show up at their assigned work site the first day or night of work. Sound familiar?

So I became a new employee one night. I showed up promptly at 6 o'clock and went through the four hours of pain. And it was painful. Several of my fellow attendees spent the time catching up on some sleep.

Now why was it so painful? Because it was a boring dissertation of information read to the attendees by an individual who, it appeared, had no interest in being there. I, along with the other attendees, were made to feel as a necessary evil to the organization. There was no variety to the presentation (more on this concept in a later chapter) as the material was read in a monotone voice. Now let me ask you, how would you like to spend four hours listening to someone lecture you on do's and don'ts of working for a company? It was easy to see why so many of the new employees became no employees the first night.

The next day was not a particular pleasant one for me. I had to ask the owner if he had ever attended one of his own orientation classes. He had not. That was where we had to begin. He attended the second night and the third day we began rewriting the entire orientation and training program for his company. Fortunately, I had an owner who listened to what needed to be done to improve, AND DID IT.

"HOW WE REMEMBER"

We have spent time discussing how adults learn but it is also very important to realize in the grand scheme of things how we as adults remember what we learn.

We have different levels of retention of information depending upon how we learn something. The more of our senses we involve in the learning process, the better chance that we will remember. For example we remember:

- □ **10% of what we read**
- □ **20% of what we hear**
- □ **30% of what we see**
- □ **50% of what we see and hear**
- □ **80% of what we say**
- □ **90% of what we say as we do**

This explains very vividly why there was such a fallout from the orientation in the company I discussed previously. After being read to all evening, they had, at best, a 20% chance at retention. With the atmosphere in which the material was presented, I venture to say the retention was much less in that particular case.

This chart will also explain to those of you who have attended my workshops why we do so many different group exercises. Actually, even for those of you who have not attended any of my workshops, the same holds true. Look again at the chart, 90% is remembered of what we say as we do. 'Nuff said.

I believe strongly that the numbers I have given you on remembering are accurate to the point that I have shaped the entire education and training part of my consulting company around this process.

In the next chapter we are going to address ways to help participants learn and remember.

Thought for the day: Ever wonder why you park your car in the driveway and drive your car in the parkway?

- Author Unknown

CHAPTER 14
EFFECTIVE LEARNING AND
REMEMBERING

Now that we have established that adults learn differently than children, let's explore some effective ways we can incorporate these adult learning principles into your training program so that your GREAT employees learn and retain the information.

"LET THE LEARNER PARTICIPATE"

The first thing I recommend you have in any workshop or seminar is round tables for the participants. It is important to have them participating in group exercises, drawing from the experiences of other people at their table. By participating in this manner they are able to express themselves with a small group and learn from that small group. Let's face it, some people just are not comfortable speaking in front of a large group but they will talk in a group of 4 or 5. Give them that opportunity and by having round tables and several group exercises they have a chance to really participate in the learning experience.

One of the other benefits of smaller group round tables is it provides the opportunity for those people who are somewhat apprehensive about speaking in larger groups to gain confidence. I know that happened in my organization. I witnessed employees who's knees were knocking when talking in front of 3 people go on to become outstanding trainers of large groups of GREAT employees.

"MAKE THE TRAINING FUN"

I found that, for the most part, the more fun we can have during the learning process the more we are going to learn. For example, don't be afraid to tell a joke on yourself. Maybe how you tried to perform a task and how you made a fool of yourself in the process. People like to know that you had to learn as well and that you weren't born knowing everything about the subject matter.

Use lots of props. I always make sure we have lots of colored magic markers and several pads of paper on an easel to write things down during the exercises I eluded to in the previous section. Change color of magic markers as you write. It is a known training fact that people like color in their classroom learning experiences.

Offer prizes for correct answers. I suggest you make up several envelopes with different bills like $5, $10, $20 and gift certificates to food stores, fast food restaurants, etc. You will be amazed at how spending just a few dollars on a few prizes will get participation in a training class. Have them draw the envelope for a great answer, etc. Don't hand it to them or it may appear you are determining who gets what prizes.

There are countless ways to have an exciting learning experience. I suggest you make it part of your training process.

By the way, I have found that people who are bashful or don't want to speak up in a group setting will all of sudden find their inner self when you start awarding cash prizes or gift certificates when they participate in the exercise. You soon find attendees asking after nearly every correct answer, "Does that qualify for a prize"? The participation is what helps along the learning process.

"USE THE EXPERIENCES OF THE LEARNER"

You may recall in our section on the differences between children and adults learning is that adults have experiences from which to draw whereas children need to accept things at face value. Here is another opportunity for you to get the participants to "get involved". For example, if you are conducting a session on customer satisfaction you may want to have an exercise that asks these questions:

1. **Write down a time when you received unusually poor service from a place of business.**

2. **Did you express your dissatisfaction to the management?**

3. **If so, was the problem resolved to your satisfaction?**

4. **Did you go back to that place of business?**

5. **Did you tell your friends and neighbors about your experience?**

This almost always will elicit a myriad of answers from the participants. They want to tell about their experience. By letting them talk about their experience you can then show them how our customers are no different. They want good service, will tell us about it, and if we don't fix it, they will tell their friends and business associates and that not only loses that customer but many potential customers we may have been able to secure. This process of using the participant's experiences is a powerful learning tool. Use it as much as you can.

One other thing---by using this method of learning you have again used a process of letting the learner participate. See how each of these ways of learning can build on each other?

"REPEAT THE IMPORTANT PARTS OF TRAINING AT LEAST 6 TIMES"

- ☐ **Always empty the vacuum bag after each use**
- ☐ **Always empty the vacuum bag after each use**
- ☐ **Always empty the vacuum bag after each use**
- ☐ **Always empty the vacuum bag after each use**
- ☐ **Always empty the vacuum bag after each use**
- ☐ **Always empty the vacuum bag after each use**

That's not exactly what I had in mind when I said repeat the important parts of training at least 6 times. The point I am making is that during the training process you want to be sure that an important part is covered 6 times in a variety of ways.

For example, using the vacuum bag illustration you obviously would say always empty the vacuum bag after each use just as I did but then you might say at a later time, "Just before you perform the task of _____you will want to be sure that the vacuum bag is emptied". Then again later during training on the vacuuming process you might say, "And the process of _____comes right after you empty the vacuum bag". Another time might be when you complete the training you would say, "And the final check list before you go home at night is to make sure you have emptied the vacuum bag".

Then when you have the employee explain AND SHOW you the process of correct vacuuming and vacuum care you will want to make sure they, and you, cover the process of emptying the vacuum bag every night after completion of the work shift.

I may have been a bit repetitive in this example but I covered it in a few paragraphs where you would cover it in a 20 minute training session on vacuuming.

Throughout the pages of this book I have repeated to you several times the key reasons why employees leave your company and what you can do to reverse that trend. By the time you reach the end you will probably have read in different ways that the main reasons GREAT employees leave your company is:

- ☐ **Nobody told them what to do**
- ☐ **Nobody compliments them on a job well done**
- ☐ **They feel there is no room for advancement**
- ☐ **Nobody trained them for their job**

So, how many times have you read the words above? Work on these main issues and you have traveled a long way in TRAINING AND KEEPING GREAT SERVICE EMPLOYEES.

"LET THE LEARNER APPLY WHAT HE/SHE HAS LEARNED"

If you recall, we said earlier that 90% of how we remember is saying it AS WE ARE DOING IT. So, when you are proceeding through the training process it is extremely important that the participant DO what you have been training.

To use the vacuuming example referred to in the previous section, after you have been through the entire process, the participant should be given the opportunity to teach back to you the operation and care of a vacuum. If they can't, we repeat the training until they can. Here is where repeating the process 6 times comes to the forefront. Maybe you'll need 8, but don't let them out of your sight until they can apply what they have learned. Remember the old adage, IF THE LEARNER HASN'T LEARNED, THE TEACHER HASN'T TAUGHT. Keep pressing forward until you are confident they are performing the task to the standard your company has established.

As a side note, you may have noticed that in presenting the Hiring Process Manual in Chapter 11, the Team Cleaning job descriptions were shown several times. This was not an error. It was designed so that the new GREAT employee was constantly reminded of the cleaning systems we were using. In addition, you may recall I also mentioned we had the Team Cleaning tasks on the walls in our applicant areas. Coincidence? Not at all.

Learning doesn't really take place if you " told them" how to do it. We tell them how, we show them how, and they show us how. Once that process is standard in your organization, training, educating AND LEARNING will take place. The by-product of what I am talking about?---TURNOVER WILL GO DOWN.

"VARY THE DELIVERY PROCESS"

Another important way for you to provide effective learning and remembering to your GREAT employees is to use a variety of teaching methods. Some examples might be:

- ☐ **Video, CD, DVD**
- ☐ **Visual demonstration**
- ☐ **Group exercises**
- ☐ **Role playing**
- ☐ **Guest presenters**
- ☐ **Wall charts and graphs**
- ☐ **Current experienced employees**

All of these are effective ways to "get the point across. In our workshops we use a variety of methods in every session. I firmly believe it helps keep everyone's interest in what we are trying to accomplish. Even if it doesn't, I'm having a lot of fun doing the workshop.

One additional key to the training and keeping GREAT employee process is having an ongoing refresher program. What in the world does that mean?

I believe it to be extremely important that the way GREAT employees continue to remain GREAT employees is to give them the opportunity to keep learning. That is why we required that EVERY employee be retrained in our new employee training process every 6 months. We gave them several options of dates to attend but made it mandatory for them to attend. They were taken through the "new employee" initial training as a refresher. By the way, all training at all times was paid.

The fact is we all get into bad habits. We can have the best intentions but sometimes we will just fall into a poor routine of doing a normal job. This mandatory refresher training every 6 months helps everyone to "get back on track". Amazing the bad habits that were picked up out in the field on some very simple tasks.

In addition, we conducted quarterly supervisory training workshops on a Saturday. We started late morning, provided either a late breakfast or did a couple hours of training, then had lunch and then a couple more hours in the afternoon. We worked hard at utilizing a variety of presentation concepts as I described earlier in this chapter. These sessions relied a great deal on the supervisors and managers for input AND presentations. It was a way for them to gain training and presentation skills.

These quarterly workshops were also where we invited those future leaders that we were told didn't exist in our work force. By us inviting them and being able to train and work with them for a day, we were able to judge for ourselves their future potential. Amazing how many "GREAT" employees we had hidden in the buildings we were cleaning.

One thing owner and managers of businesses would do well to learn at an early age is that they do not have a monopoly on knowledge. Owning the business does not make you the expert on the technical aspects of your business. Your employees already know that and it is best if you learn it soon as well. Let them learn and demonstrate their skills through regular training and educational seminars and workshops. You are building their self confidence and self esteem and they are helping you build a GREAT company.

Thought for the day: **Marriage is called an institution, but then so are Alcatraz and Leavenworth.**

- Author Unknown

CHAPTER 15

OTHER KEEPING IDEAS THAT WORK

By now you have probably realized that I believe that the way to keep GREAT employees is to show them how to do what they are being asked to do, compliment them on a job well done, and be sure that they are always aware of the opportunities for career advancement with your organization.

But there are some additional ways to keep GREAT employees and you have probably been thinking about them as you have been reading this book. So what are some of them?

COMPETITIVE PAY---Absolutely has to be part of the process. It is no secret that if you are in the Building Service or related business, that you are not going to be competing with the factories and offices in the wage war. That is why I believe it is so important to do the things I have been discussing in the previous chapters. You can however, have your pay scale be at the top end of the industry for your market area. My philosophy was and is, that maybe we CAN'T compete with the factories and offices in wages, but we can create a family atmosphere that they can't, and if the GREAT people we employ choose to be in this industry, we will pay them at the top end of the scale. This coupled with addressing the reasons why people leave our industry will provide us the advantage.

RECOGNITION—Taking the time to recognize your GREAT employees is another way to let them know how important they are to your company. Remembering their anniversary with your company and their birthday is important. How about securing their spouse's birth date and sending a card to them at their home? Their wedding anniversary? Perfect attendance, recognition in the company newsletter. Work they have done in their church or synagogue, with the boys or girls club, the cleaning for a reason foundation, etc. Very important. It is also important to many of your customers.

COMPANY NEWSLETTER---I mentioned this in the recruiting section and want to reiterate the importance here of a company newsletter in every language that your employees communicate in. We had a monthly letter that went to all employees, customers, key prospective customers, and my Mom. There were times that I wondered if the newsletter was even being read until we would accidentally forget to mention someone's birthday or anniversary. Believe me, they read it even if they tell you they don't.

One side benefit of the company newsletter. I learned from some of my customers that they read it to see if any of the GREAT employees I had working in their building were having a birthday and if so, they would leave a card for them on the desk at night. You think that didn't strike a positive chord with the GREAT employee working in that building.

I also secured some major clients by sending the newsletter to prospects on my "Hit List". I can recall receiving a call from the manager of a large medical facility who said, "I am looking through your newsletter and it appears you do so much more than the average janitorial service when it comes to employee recognition and training that I would like to talk to you about cleaning our facility. Are you interested in coming to see me?" Well, let's see, was I interested? I guess we were able to fit one more customer into our portfolio.

I should mention here that we published our monthly training calendar for each district office in the newsletter so our employees, customers, and prospects were aware of upcoming events and could attend at any time.

ANNUAL FAMILY PICNIC EVENTS---This became one of the most anticipated events in several of our districts. I will tell you it began slow and built over several years. It also did not work in one or two of the districts because the managers did not embrace it as they could or should have. Guess which of my districts had the highest turnover?

The key to the success of this event is to involve as many people as possible in the planning of the event. The company can provide the major expense items but we found inviting the employees to bring their favorite dish was the most successful. Not only that, but I learned to eat and like a lot of food of different cultures. Many times my stomach did not enjoy it as much as I did but what great experiences they were.

Another key to success of the family picnic event is to provide entertainment for the children. Magicians, clowns, face painters were always a hit and relatively inexpensive. I know I enjoyed them.

HOLIDAY OPEN HOUSES—These were a hit in many of my districts, again to the degree that the manager in charge promoted them. Our pay days were the 15th and last day of the month so in December, the 15th was also used for a Christmas open house—again with the employees having the opportunity to bring their favorite dish---oooh my stomach.

One of my managers would have a special seat decorated and reserved just for Santa. At a designated time Santa would arrive and each of the children got to sit on Santa's lap and have their picture taken and given a small gift that my manager, along with his wife had picked up at Target or Walmart. It wasn't important what the gift was, rather that there was one. I even got to sit on Santa's lap. Poor guy. (Santa)

The important part of this whole event was the next week after the open house we would make the rounds to the various buildings and present the employees with the pictures that had been taken of their children on Santa's lap. It was a great experience for all of us.

You can see by the examples above that there are many different events you can hold that help to KEEP GREAT EMPLOYEES.

As a side story to the holiday open house, the Santa that we used in the one district, through circumstances unrelated to his employment performance, had to leave our company. But he called each year to ask if he could still be Santa because he enjoyed being around the people and the kids. He was our Santa for many years. It also helped that he spoke more than one language.

The whole purpose of this chapter is to get you thinking of ways that you may not be using now that help to KEEP GREAT EMPLOYEES. Whenever I do this group exercise in my workshops, we have an abundance of great ideas that are presented. Many times people, and maybe you as well, think that these events are expensive. You will be surprised at how creative your staff can be on things to do that invest little or none of the company funds. Remember you do not have a monopoly on good ideas.

Thought for the day: **A big shot is nothing more than a little shot who kept on shooting.**

-   Author Unknown

CHAPTER 16

YOUR PLAN OF ACTION

So, we've spent some time together talking about the different ways we can find GREAT service employees, how to effectively bring them on board, and the reasons why they leave your organization or choose to stay.

Now it's your turn. I want you to be able to make positive changes in your company as a result of reading this book. I never like my workshop participants leaving without a plan of action.

Incidentally, if you are thinking, why is he having me do all this? Is he just trying to take up lots of paper? Let me remind you, that every time you turn over an employee, you have just thrown $500 plus down the drain. Doesn't it make sense to let me use up some paper and you to use up some lead or ink and write down a plan of action?

So here goes your opportunity to preserve your cash.

DO YOU PLAN TO BEGIN RECUITING INSTEAD OF HIRING YOUR FUTURE GREAT EMPLOYEES? IF SO, HOW? IF NOT, WHY NOT?

WHAT WAYS CAN MY ORGANIZATION UTILIZE:

Newspaper ads-----

Career fairs-----

Neighborhood door hangars-----

Headhunting-----

Business cards-----

Strip malls-----

Ethnic radio stations-----

Flea markets-----

On line recruiting-----

Other methods-----

HOW DO I PLAN TO MANAGE THE RECRUITING PROCESS?

Software----

Newsletters-----

Other-----

WHAT ACTION DO I NEED TO TAKE TO IMPROVE THE APPEARANCE OF MY FACILITIES?

Outside-----

Inside-----

HOW DO I PLAN TO CHANGE MY INTERVIEWING PROCESS, IF I DO?

Our attitude towards prospective GREAT employees-----

The questions I ask------

HOW DO I PLAN TO CHANGE THE WAY WE PROVIDE ORIENTATION TO NEW POTENTIAL GREAT EMPLOYEES?

Orientation video/DVD-----

Hiring process manual-----

New employee checklist-----

Updated job descriptions----

HOW DO I PLAN TO CHANGE MY TRAINING PROCESS?

Communication procedure-----

Making it fun------

Making it for adult learning-----

Repeating it_____times so we are sure the learner has learned-----

WHAT ARE SOME OTHER NEW IDEAS WE ARE GOING TO IMPLEMENT TO ASSURE THAT OUR GREAT EMPLOYEES STAY?

The biggest investment you make in your company is the one you make in your GREAT employees. They truly are the inventory you have to provide to your customers. I encourage you to do everything you can to protect those valuable assets. It truly can be a wonderful experience. It was and still is for me.

Thought for the day: The secret to successful managing is to keep those who hate you away from those who are undecided.

-   Casey Stengel

CHAPTER 17

SAMPLE JOB DESCRIPTIONS

This is a compilation of several sample job descriptions for a Building Service Contracting Company. Use them where you can but again, I recommend you get professional advice.

An important part of any job description is a task that says "Other duties as assigned". That is the "catch all" phrase that eliminates the response from an unhappy worker who says "that's not in my job description".

I developed a saying many years ago that was, "If you say that's not your job, the one you have won't be for long either".

Anyway, I hope these job descriptions and the other ideas contained in this book are helpful to you.

ENJOY THE JOURNEY!

NOTE: The job descriptions shown in this chapter along with the hiring process manual information shown in Chapter 11 can be ordered on CD from our web site at www.consultantsincleaning.com.

Your Company Name
Staff Position Description and Specifications
Revised Effective _____

Corporate Human Resource Coordinator   Page __ of __

POSITION TITLE: Corporate Human Resource Coordinator

SUPERVISED BY: Vice President

DEFINITION:

The Corporate Human Resource Coordinator (HR Coordinator) is responsible for the successful administration of the philosophy, policies and procedures relating to all personnel at *Your Company Name*. The final result required is a high morale people-oriented organization operating by the rules.

MINIMUM QUALIFICATIONS:

1. Experience with popular word processing program required. Microsoft Word for Windows preferred.

2. Ability to communicate in Spanish required, both oral and written required.

3. Database experience helpful. ACT II and Microsoft Access preferred.

4. Spreadsheet experience helpful. Microsoft Excel preferred.

5. Desktop publishing experience helpful. Microsoft Publisher preferred.

6. Basic bookkeeping concepts helpful.

7. Familiar with Occupational Safety Health Administration (OSHA) and Mine Safety Health Administration (MSHA) safety rules and regulations.

8. Valid driver's license and good driving record.

9. Basic knowledge of Worker's Compensation law and rules including calculation of the Modification Factor required.

10. Basic knowledge of Employment and Unemployment laws and rules required.

11. Ability to effectively deal with customers, employees, potential employees, and regulating government representatives essential.

PHYSICAL REQUIREMENTS:

Visual acuity to the extent that the person can use a PC for creating, editing, and proof reading documents, spreadsheets, etc. Hearing/speaking ability in English and Spanish to the extent that the person can converse with customers, employees, and prospective employees in person and on the telephone. Ability to develop and conduct training programs. Ability to the extent that the person can identify safety hazards such as frayed cords, wet floors, etc. Ability to converse over the phone with District Managers, OSHA personnel, INS personnel, insurance company representatives, etc. Because demonstration is the preferred method of instruction, and on occasion involving new job starts (most commonly during start-ups of larger jobs), the incumbent must be able to lift 40 pounds and perform cleaning duties involving lifting, standing, bending and twisting.

JOB LOCATION:

Headquarters in the Corporate Office. Locations and times of work will vary by need in all Districts. Travel to all District/ Project locations as needed.

AREAS OF RESPONSIBILITY:

1. Job descriptions.

2. Recruitment (advertising, interviewing, drug testing, background checks.)

3. Equal Employment Opportunity (EEO) compliance.

4. Wage/Hour compliance.

5. Orientation - preliminary.

6. Safety - Worker's Compensation – Insurance / Bonding.

7. Training development (preliminary and on-going in conduction with department needs.)

8. Unemployment (training, hearings, record maintenance and management.)

9. I-9 verification.

10. OSHA and MSHA:

    a. Hazard Communication.

    b. Bloodborne Pathogens Standards.

    c. Right to know.

11. Personnel Policies and Procedures:

    a. Development.

    b. Monitoring implementation.

    c. Enforcement.

d. Discipline.

e. Benefit Administration.

f. Group Health/COBRA.

g. Payroll Deduction Plan.

h. Employment Tax Credit Program.

i. Right to Know.

j. Newsletter.

k. Employee Relations (complaints, investigations, etc.)

l. Sexual Harassment.

m. Attendance Record Retention.

n. Termination Records, etc.

o. Material Safety Data Sheets (MSDS) (coordination and enforcement.)

p. All accident investigations in cooperation with operations.

q. Americans with Disabilities Act (ADA.)

r. Operations - Human Resource Control.

s. Uniform Control - new and exiting employees.

t. Identification badges.

u. Customer / job site investigation - Operations.

v. Safety Manual.

DUTIES:

1. Receives position requests from District Manager and/or Production Supervisor and acts to fill vacancies in as prompt and effective manner as possible.

2. Makes decisions on placement of job advertisements with print, electronic (radio, TV, etc.) and any other media.

3. Oversees the hiring of District personnel for positions needed by using Company established procedures to include an initial interview and complete orientation. Only those candidates who are qualified, based on the HR departments judgment will be considered for employment.

4. Oversees the maintenance of daily records of all job openings in the District as requests are placed and oversees the maintenance of records of those filled positions.

5. Oversees the completion of all (entire Company) necessary employment paperwork to assure it is accurate and complete; i.e. signatures, I-9's, proper ID, Social Security numbers, uniform and Company policies.

6. Oversees that all applicants' applications hired on current day have the *Your Company Name* Post Hire Form filled out and turned in to the Corporate Office on the same day. Insures that a typed badge and uniform is given to each new employee.

7. Oversees the instruction and material to new employees so that the new employee can arrive at the job site with a minimum of problems. Coordinates with District Managers so that the new employee is received and properly started.

8. Compiles information for monthly newsletter. Items to be entered in newsletter each time: birthdays (staff & regular), employees who received special recognition, President's message, supply items (District Managers), Employee of

the Month (or months), new staff employees (if any), staff promotions (if any), and humor items.

9. Prints, translates, edits newsletter and sends to an outside source to have copies made.

10. Keeps newsletter mailing list up to date.

11. Encourages employees to submit articles for publication.

12. Keep the personnel office neat and organized at all times.

13. Oversees the basic training for new employee for the job that he/she is hired to do.

14. Discusses policy books/pamphlets that are needed for Human Resources and Personnel with Vice President and orders upon approval.

15. Visits the job site where accidents occur in *State* and writes up and follows up with all Worker's Compensation claims. Oversees the completion of the same in all other states.

16. Keeps records of all employees hired through special agencies where there is an opportunity of financial reimbursement of part of their hours.

17. Oversees the making and distribution and control of I.D. badges for the entire Company.

18. Maintains a database of all prospective employees and maintains ongoing communications with them through letters, Company newsletter mailings, telephone and other communications needed to encourage the prospective employee to make *Your Company Name* their choice of employment.

19. Purchases and maintains accurate records of uniform items (shirts, caps, jackets) for all locations. Assists the President in selection of uniform design, vendors, etc.

20. Coordinates all group insurance programs, claims benefit explanation, enrollment, termination's, COBRA, etc.

21. Coordinates all unemployment claims, responses, investigations, hearings, appeals, etc.

22. Conducts regular ongoing safety inspections in all *State* buildings being maintained by *Your Company Name*. Written reports of these inspections are to be submitted to the Vice President on a weekly basis. A minimum of four (4) site visits and inspections are required weekly.

23. Help other departments as needed.

ORGANIZATIONAL RELATIONSHIPS:

The Corporate Human Resource Coordinator is supervised by the Vice President for assignment, guidance, evaluation and problem solving. Since there is daily telephone and in-person contact with applicants and *Your Company Name* employees, a harmonious and cooperative attitude must be maintained.

NOTE:

Job/Position Descriptions are written to give employees and supervisors information about the job. They are not contracts of any kind. Employees can be reassigned at any time and given other duties within the Corporation. Not all jobs have position descriptions. It is impossible to list each and every duty in a position description. Other duties may be assigned.

Your Company Name
Staff Position Description and Specifications
Revised Effective _____
District Manager   Page ___ of ___

POSITION TITLE: District Manager

REPORTS TO: President & Vice President

DEFINITION:

1. The District Manager is responsible for all *Your Company Name* operations (plan, organize, direct, and control operational, sales, and administrative activities) within his or her geographic area.

2. A District may be responsible for several geographical locations with sales under $1 million per year in annual revenue, or a single location with sales more than $1 million per year in annual revenue.

3. The final result required is a high-morale people-oriented organization operating by the policies that meet or exceed customer expectations while achieving specific quality and profit objectives.

MINIMUM QUALIFICATIONS:

1. Experience as a Production Supervisor or comparable position in a contract cleaning or service-oriented company. Registered Building Service Manager (RBSM) preferred.

2. Must have a valid driver's license and good driving record.

PHYSICAL REQUIREMENTS:

Visual acuity to the extent that the person can see dirt on floors, windows improperly cleaned, dust on tables, etc. Hearing/speaking ability in English and in some cases, another language, to the extent that the person can converse with employees and prospective employees in person and on the telephone. Hearing/speaking/ writing ability to communicate with customers in English. The ability to conduct staff meetings and training classes. Ability to the extent that the person can identify safety hazards such as frayed cords, wet floors, lifting hazards, etc. Because demonstration is the preferred method of instruction, and on occasion involving new job starts (most commonly during start-ups of larger jobs), the incumbent must be able to lift 40 pounds and perform cleaning duties involving lifting, standing, bending and twisting.

JOB LOCATION:

Headquarters in the District office. Locations and times of work will vary by need in all locations. Travel to all District/project locations as needed.

DUTIES:

The District Manager is responsible for directing all *Your Company Name* activities within his or her geographic area in accordance with *Your Company Name* policies and procedures. These include:

1. Recruitment.

2. Human Resources.

3. Office Administration.

4. Building Services Account Management.

5. Tag and Special Services.

6. Budgeting.

7. Offensive and Defensive Marketing.

8. Safety.

9. Customer Relations.

10. Training and Evaluation.

11. Logistics.

MAJOR GOALS:

1. To manage *Your Company Name's* District effectively and to develop new goals and objectives within the realm of our business.

2. To deliver the product or service to meet or exceed our customers' needs, expectations and standards.

3. To develop key personnel and strive to ensure their success.

SUBORDINATE GOALS AND KEY RESULTS:

1. To provide direction and support, *Your Company Name* District management personnel and the District Manager will be successful in this Key Results Area when:

   a. All new staff members are trained and managing their area self-sufficiently.

   b. Customer relations calls and written Job Status Reports are accomplished according to standard procedures.

c.   An individual is designated to train new personnel in safety, product and equipment knowledge and operating procedures.

d.   Labor and material operating percentages are maintained at or below budgeted percentages.

e.   Revenue projections are achieved.

f.   Managers are given the opportunity to take advantage of available training in the area of building maintenance service within budgetary constraints.

g.   Managerial personnel understand their roles and each is performing in a satisfactory manner.

h.   Personally make customer relations calls on the top 10 customers in the District on a predetermined scheduled basis.

i.   Personally conduct Safety Audits of assigned accounts.

2.   To provide direction to Tag and Special sales in order to achieve sales goals and profitability, the District Manager will be successful in this Key Results Area when:

a.   He/she is effective in the areas of job estimates and scheduling.

b.   A dependable support staff of workers is developed and trained.

c.   A solid reputation of good service is developed within the District geographical area.

d.   He/she attains budgeted revenue and profitability projections.

3. To designate time each week to plan or review goals and objectives, the District Manager will be successful in this Key Results Area when:

   a. At least 40% of the Manager's time is spent in planning, goal setting, organizing and performing administrative functions necessary to perform his/her job satisfactorily.

   b. Delegation of short range goals and day to day activities has been done.

   c. He/she holds monthly sales meetings.

   d. Subordinates prepare job results descriptions.

   e. He/she is able to readjust plans as needed to achieve annual goals.

4. To develop a District organizational chart and make allowances for growth, the District Manager will be successful in this Key Results Area when:

   a. An organizational chart is prepared.

   b. Production Supervisors and Site Supervisors work as a team.

   c. Managers reflect a positive attitude.

   d. A designated percentage of his/her time is equally divided between revenue centers and support activities.

5. To assist all department heads in achieving their goals and develop positive attitudes, the District Manager will be successful in this Key Results Area when:

a. All management personnel are regularly given the opportunity to evaluate and improve operational processes.

b. Managers focus on fiscal goals and objectives and have a true understanding of the part they play in the overall picture.

c. Management personnel reflect a positive image of themselves and the Company.

6. To monitor financial and service results in each sub-area, the District Manager will be successful in this Key Results Area when:

a. Managers properly use the Budget Comparison Report and Pay Period Master reports on a <u>daily</u> basis.

b. Managers properly ensure that each employee receives an accurate and timely error-free paycheck on the scheduled pay date, i.e. no hand checks.

c. He/she reviews Profit and Loss statements, Trend Reports, and tracks fiscal budget figures.

d. He/she reviews Job Status Reports, public relations calls and individual account material usage.

e. He/she continues to compare all operating costs and overhead percentages within Building Service Contractor's Association International (BSCAI) Industrial Performance Standards and takes corrective action where necessary.

f. Administrative functions are performed in accordance with corporate office instructions.

7. To monitor sales efforts to ensure sales and marketing goals are met, the District Manager will be successful in this Key Results Area when:

   a. He/she has identified potential target accounts in the area.

   b. He/she has developed a marketing plan with the *Your Company Name* President.

   c. New sales are closed within margin guidelines.

   d. He/she participates in local civic organizations as directed by the *Your Company Name* Vice President and/or President.

   e. He/she tracks lost accounts for re-marketing.

   f. He/she spends 20 to 25% of their time on sales activities.

8. To achieve zero lost time on accidents in the District, and to be in compliance with all Occupational Safety Health Administration (OSHA) and/or Mine Safety Health Administration (MSHA) requirements, the District Manager will be successful in this Key Results Area when:

   a. All subordinate Supervisors actively support the safety program and enforce the provisions.

   b. Material Safety Data Sheets (MSDS) are on hand in each account and are current.

   c. All employees receive the required training.

   d. All employees use the required safety equipment.

    e. Safety is a factor in considering equipment or chemical purchase recommendations.

    f. Accidents are promptly reported and investigated.

    g. Accident investigation reports include practical steps to prevent reoccurrence.

    h. Monthly District safety meetings are held.

    i. A responsible person is designated as the District Safety Director.

9. To properly administer personnel policies, the District Manager will have been successful in this Key Results Area when:

    a. Employee grievances are at a minimum.

    b. No complaints are filed with city, county, state, or federal Equal Employment Opportunity Commission (EEOC) offices. (And if complaints are filed, *Your Company Name* prevails in subsequent judgments).

    c. Disciplinary actions are timely, proper, and documented in accordance with company policy.

    d. Interviewing and hiring actions are proper.

    e. Personnel files are accurate.

    f. Entries in the personnel master file are accurate and timely.

    g. Equal Employment Opportunity (EEO) and Affirmative Action policies are implemented.

10. To ensure that any subcontractors have suitable insurance and that the subcontractor's performance

is monitored, the District Manager will have been successful in this Key Results Area when:

a. Appropriate certificates of insurance are obtained on subcontractors.

b. Subcontractor's performance is monitored for suitability and actions taken when performance is below par.

11. To ensure that logistical controls are established for supplies, equipment and tools, the District Manager will have been successful in this Key Results Area when:

a. Account Operations Manual and procedures are established at each account.

b. Cleaning supplies are identified and established as authorized for each account.

c. Inventory levels are established for each account and reorder procedures are established.

d. Equipment and tools are accounted for and maintained in a clean and operational manner.

e. Key control procedures are established and monitored.

ORGANIZATIONAL RELATIONSHIPS:

The District Manager is supervised by the Vice President and/or President for assignment, guidance, evaluation and problem solving. Since there is daily telephone and in-person contact with internal and external customers, a harmonious and cooperative attitude must be maintained.

NOTE:

Job/Position Descriptions are written to give employees and supervisors information about the job. They are not contracts of any kind. Employees can be reassigned at any time and given other duties within the corporation. Not all jobs have position descriptions. It is impossible to list each and every duty in a position description. Other duties may be assigned.

Your Company Name
Staff Position Description and Specifications
Revised Effective _____

Project Manager   Page __ of __

POSITION TITLE: Project Manager

REPORTS TO: District Manager. Also responds to requests/
instructions from the customer.

DEFINITION:

1. A Project Manager is responsible for all maintenance
   tasks within an account.

2. A Project Manager may supervise one large account
   within the District location, or a large geographically
   separated unit.

3. The Project Manager interviews and hires the crew.
   The Project Manager is responsible for training and
   supervision.

4. The Project Manager also interfaces with the customer
   to ensure customer satisfaction with our work. The
   overall goal and first priority of the Project Manager is
   to become an important resource for the customer. He
   or she is to have the best interests of the customer in
   mind for all scheduling decisions.

5. The final result required is a high-morale people-
   oriented organization operating by the policies that
   meet or exceed customer expectations while achieving
   specific quality and profit objectives.

MINIMUM QUALIFICATIONS:

1. Experience in building maintenance operations. Prefer
   experience managing large cleaning crews.

2. Good people skills.

3. Ability to interface with customer personnel is essential.

4. Registered Building Service Manager (RBSM) preferred.

5. Must have valid driver's license and good driving record.

PHYSICAL REQUIREMENTS:

Visual acuity to the extent that the person can see dirt on floors, windows improperly cleaned, dust on tables, etc. Hearing/speaking ability in English, and in some cases, another language, to the extent that the person can converse with employees and prospective employees in person and on the telephone. Hearing/speaking/ writing ability to communicate with customers in English. The ability to conduct staff meetings and training classes. Ability to the extent that the person can identify safety hazards such as frayed cords, wet floors, lifting hazards, etc. Because demonstration is the preferred method of instruction, and on occasion involving new job starts (most commonly during start-ups of larger jobs), the incumbent must be able to lift 40 pounds and perform cleaning duties involving lifting, standing, bending and twisting.

JOB LOCATION:

Headquarters in the major Project. Locations and time of work will vary by need in all locations. Travel to District and Project locations as needed.

DUTIES:

1. Ensures that the work identified in the specifications is performed properly, on time, safely and within the budget.

2. Schedules and coordinates custodial duties, and current services with the customer.

3. Prepares schedule and supervises work assignments for all personnel.

4. Inspects work of subordinates.

5. Uses computer products to track work.

6. Conducts training for *Your Company Name* employees.

7. Orders all cleaning supplies and equipment. Maintains security of all tools, equipment and supplies.

8. Administers the *Your Company Name* Safety Program at the account.

9. Administers *Your Company Name* personnel policies in accordance with *Your Company Name* Personnel Policy Manual.

10. Prepares required reports.

11. Enforces the account/District dress code.

12. Responds daily to requests from the customer.

13. Completes all work in a professional manner commensurate with industry and safety standards.

14. Any other duties as assigned.

MAJOR GOALS:

1. To manage *Your Company Name's* Project effectively and to develop new goals and objectives within the realm of our business.

2. To achieve required margin levels.

3. To deliver the product or service to meet or exceed our customers' needs, expectations and standards.

4. To develop key personnel and strive to ensure their success.

SUBORDINATE GOALS AND KEY RESULTS:

1. To continue to improve customer relations, the Project Manager will be successful in this Key Results Area when:

   a. A contact schedule is established with major tenants/ executives and the schedule is followed. (Applicable if tenant contact is encouraged.)

   b. The customer is encouraged to contact him/her when issues arise.

   c. The Customer Communications Log Book is read daily. Action items are acted upon, corrections/work checked, and action documented in the log and, when appropriate, verbally to the client contact.

   d. Customer complaints and concerns are successfully resolved within the time period agreed upon.

   e. The account is inspected during or subsequent to each client meeting.

   f. Immediate Attention Forms are given to and acted upon by Supervisors or Lead People.

   g. All changes in account cleaning specifications or procedures are reduced to writing with copies to the Corporate Office and the client within three working days of the change.

2. To develop Supervisors and potential Supervisors, the Project Manager will be successful in this Key Results Area when:

   a. Cleaning specialists have been trained on their assigned duties.

   b. All current Supervisors have completed the *Your Company Name* Supervisory Development Course.

   c. All Supervisors attend quarterly meetings.

   d. Potential Supervisors are identified and afforded the opportunity to complete the *Your Company Name* Supervisory Development Course.

3. To maintain operational control of the account, the Project Manager will be successful in this Key Results Area when:

   a. The account file is established and maintained.

   b. The Account Operations Manual is up-to-date.

   c. Project Scheduling is established and maintained.

   d. Cleaning supplies are identified and established as authorized for each account.

   e. Inventory levels are established for each account and reorder procedures are established.

   f. Equipment and tools are accounted for and maintained in a clean and operational manner.

   g. Key control procedures are established and monitored.

   h. Job costs are analyzed and planning is implemented to continue to maintain costs at the budgeted level.

    i.   The Budget Comparison Report and Pay Period Master reports are used on a <u>daily</u> basis.

    j.   Inspections and walkthroughs continue to insure that tasks are being completed in a timely, workmanlike manner using Job Status Report.

4. To develop management skills through active participation in development opportunities, the Project Manager will be successful in the Key Results Area when:

    a.   He/she has completed the RBSM course of study.

    b.   He/she has received the RBSM Certification.

5. To improve employee job satisfaction, the Project Manager will be successful in this Key Results Area when:

    a.   He/she properly ensures that each employee receives an accurate and timely error-free paycheck on the scheduled pay date, i.e. no hand checks.

    b.   Absenteeism and turnover are minimal.

    c.   The Project Manager seeks out and compliments at least one employee for a job well done.

6. To explore growth opportunities, the Project Manager will be successful in this Key Results Area when:

    a.   New services or expansion of current services have been identified and suggested to the client.

    b.   During the year, one new service has been added to the account.

7. To create a safe work place, the Project Manager will be successful in this Key Results Area when:

    a. All subordinate Supervisors actively support the safety program and enforce the provisions.

    b. Material Safety Data Sheets (MSDS) are on hand in each account and are current.

    c. All employees receive the required training.

    d. All employees use the required safety equipment.

    e. Safety is a factor in considering equipment or chemical purchases.

    f. Accidents are promptly reported and investigated in accordance with Project/District/Company policies.

    g. Accident investigation reports include practical steps to prevent reoccurrence.

8. To properly administer personnel policies, the incumbent will have been successful in the Key Results Area when:

    a. Employee grievances are at a minimum.

    b. No complaints are filed with city, county, state or federal Equal Employment Opportunity Commission (EEOC) offices. (And, if complaints are filed, *Your Company Name* prevails in subsequent judgments.)

    c. Discipline is timely, proper and documented in accordance with Company policy.

    d. Interviewing and hiring are done on site.

        (1) I-9 forms are properly completed.

    (2)   **Police checks are properly conducted.**

    (3)   **Hiring documents are completed and distributed to the Corporate Office on a timely basis.**

ORGANIZATIONAL RELATIONSHIPS:

The Project Manager is supervised by the District Manager/President for assignment, guidance, evaluation and problem solving. Since there is daily telephone and in-person contact with internal and external customers, a harmonious and cooperative attitude must be maintained.

NOTE:

Job/Position Descriptions are written to give employees and supervisors information about the job. They are not contracts of any kind. Employees can be reassigned at any time, and given other duties within the corporation. Not all jobs have position descriptions. It is impossible to list each and every duty in a position description and employees are expected to follow the instructions of their supervisor whether or not those instructions are included in a job description.

Your Company Name
Staff Position Description and Specifications
Revised Effective _____

Operations Manager   Page __ of __

POSITION TITLE: Operations Manager

REPORTS TO: District Manager. Also responds to requests/
instructions from the customer.

DEFINITION:

1. An Operations Manager is responsible for all maintenance tasks within all accounts in the District.

2. The Operations Manager interviews and hires the crew. The Operations Manager is responsible for training and supervision.

3. The Operations Manager also interfaces with the customer to ensure customer satisfaction with our work. The overall goal and first priority of the Operations Manager is to become an important resource for the customer. He or she is to have the best interests of the customer in mind for all scheduling decisions.

4. The final result required is a high-morale people-oriented organization operating by the policies that meet or exceed customer expectations while achieving specific quality and profit objectives.

MINIMUM QUALIFICATIONS:

1. Experience in building maintenance operations. Prefer experience managing large cleaning crews.

2. Good people skills.

3. Ability to interface with customer personnel is essential.

4. Registered Building Service Manager (RBSM) preferred.

5. Must have valid driver's license and good driving record.

PHYSICAL REQUIREMENTS:

Visual acuity to the extent that the person can see dirt on floors, windows improperly cleaned, dust on tables, etc. Hearing/speaking ability in English, and in some cases, another language, to the extent that the person can converse with employees and prospective employees in person and on the telephone. Hearing/speaking/writing ability to communicate with customers in English. The ability to conduct staff meetings and training classes. Ability to the extent that the person can identify safety hazards such as frayed cords, wet floors, lifting hazards, etc. Because demonstration is the preferred method of instruction, and on occasion involving new job starts (most commonly during start-ups of larger jobs), the incumbent must be able to lift 40 pounds and perform cleaning duties involving lifting, standing, bending and twisting.

JOB LOCATION:

Headquarters in the major District. Locations and time of work will vary by need in all locations.

DUTIES:

1. Ensures that the work identified in the specifications is performed properly, on time, safely and within the budget.

2. Schedules and coordinates custodial duties, and current services with the customer.

3. Prepares schedule and supervises work assignments for all personnel.

4. Inspects work of subordinates.

5. Uses computer products to track work.

6. Conducts training for *Your Company Name* employees.

7. Maintains security of all tools, equipment and supplies.

8. Administers the *Your Company Name* Safety Program.

9. Administers *Your Company Name* personnel policies in accordance with *Your Company Name* Personnel Policy Manual.

10. Prepares required reports.

11. Enforces the District dress code.

12. Responds daily to requests from the customer.

13. Completes all work in a professional manner commensurate with industry and safety standards.

14. Any other duties as assigned.

MAJOR GOALS:

1. To manage *Your Company Name's* Project effectively and to develop new goals and objectives within the realm of our business.

2. To achieve required margin levels.

3. To deliver the product or service to meet or exceed our customers' needs, expectations and standards.

4. To develop key personnel and strive to ensure their success.

SUBORDINATE GOALS AND KEY RESULTS:

1. To continue to improve customer relations, the Operations Manager will be successful in this Key Results Area when:

    a. A contact schedule is established with major tenants/executives and the schedule is followed. (Applicable if tenant contact is encouraged.)

    b. The customer is encouraged to contact him/her when issues arise.

    c. The Customer Communications Log Book is read daily. Action items are acted upon, corrections/work checked, and action documented in the log, and when appropriate, verbally to the client contact.

    d. Customer complaints and concerns are successfully resolved within the time period agreed upon.

    e. The accounts are inspected during each client meeting.

    f. Immediate Attention Forms are given to and acted upon by Supervisors or Lead People.

    g. All changes in account cleaning specifications or procedures are reduced to writing with copies to the Corporate Office and the client within three working days of the change.

2. To develop Supervisors and potential Supervisors, the Operations Manager will be successful in this Key Results Area when:

    a. Cleaning specialists have been trained on their assigned duties.

b. All current Supervisors have completed the *Your Company Name* Supervisory Development Course.

c. All Supervisors attend quarterly meetings.

d. Potential Supervisors are identified and afforded the opportunity to complete the *Your Company Name* Supervisory Development Course.

3. To maintain operational control of accounts, the Operations Manager will be successful in this Key Results Area when:

a. All account files are established and maintained.

b. The Account Operations Manual is up-to-date.

c. Project Scheduling is established and maintained.

d. Cleaning supplies are identified and established as authorized for each account.

e. Inventory levels are established for each account and reorder procedures are established.

f. Equipment and tools are accounted for and maintained in a clean and operational manner.

g. Key control procedures are established and monitored.

h. Job costs are analyzed and planning is implemented to continue to maintain costs at the budgeted level.

i. The Budget Comparison Report and Pay Period Master reports are used on a <u>daily</u> basis.

j. Inspections and walkthroughs continue to insure that tasks are being completed in a timely, workmanlike manner using Job Status Report.

4. To develop management skills through active participation in development opportunities, the Operations Manager will be successful in the Key Results Area when:

   a. He/she has completed the RBSM course of study.

   b. He/she has received the RBSM Certification.

5. To improve employee job satisfaction, the Operations Manager will be successful in this Key Results Area when:

   a. He/she properly ensures that each employee receives an accurate and timely error-free paycheck on the scheduled pay date, i.e. no hand checks.

   b. Absenteeism and turnover are minimal.

   c. The Operations Manager seeks out and compliments at least one employee for a job well done.

6. To explore growth opportunities, the Operations Manager will be successful in this Key Results Area when:

   a. New services or expansion of current services have been identified and suggested to the client.

   b. During the year, one new service has been added to several accounts.

7. To create a safe work place, the Operations Manager will be successful in this Key Results Area when:

   a. All subordinate Supervisors actively support the safety program and enforce the provisions.

    b. Material Safety Data Sheets (MSDS) are on hand in each account and are current.

    c. All employees receive the required training.

    d. All employees use the required safety equipment.

    e. Safety is a factor in considering equipment or chemical purchases.

    f. Accidents are promptly reported and investigated in accordance with Project/District/Company policies.

    g. Accident investigation reports include practical steps to prevent reoccurrence.

8. To properly administer personnel policies, the incumbent will have been successful in the Key Results Area when:

    a. Employee grievances are at a minimum.

    b. No complaints are filed with city, county, state or federal Equal Employment Opportunity Commission (EEOC) offices. (And, if complaints are filed, *Your Company Name* prevails in subsequent judgments.)

    c. Discipline is timely, proper and documented in accordance with Company policy.

    d. Interviewing and hiring are done.

        (1) I-9 forms are properly completed.

        (2) Police checks are properly conducted.

        (3) Hiring documents are completed and distributed to the Corporate Office on a timely basis.

ORGANIZATIONAL RELATIONSHIPS:

The Operations Manager is supervised by the District Manager/ President for assignment, guidance, evaluation and problem solving. Since there is daily telephone and in-person contact with internal and external customers, a harmonious and cooperative attitude must be maintained.

NOTE:

Job/Position Descriptions are written to give employees and supervisors information about the job. They are not contracts of any kind. Employees can be reassigned at any time, and given other duties within the corporation. Not all jobs have position descriptions. It is impossible to list each and every duty in a position description and employees are expected to follow the instructions of their supervisor whether or not those instructions are included in a job description.

Your Company Name
Staff Position Description and Specifications
Revised Effective _____
Production Supervisor   **Page __ of __**

POSITION TITLE: Production Supervisor

REPORTS TO: District Manager

DEFINITION:

1. The Production Supervisor is responsible for all maintenance tasks within one or several accounts.

2. In some District locations, the Production Supervisor may interview and hire the crew. In other locations, they conduct second interviews and make hiring decisions after an initial interview/screening.

3. In all locations, the Production Supervisor is responsible for training and supervision.

4. In all locations, the Production Supervisor interfaces with the customer to ensure customer satisfaction with our work.

5. The final result required is a high-morale people-oriented organization operating by the rules that meet or exceeds customer expectations while achieving specific quality and profit objectives.

MINIMUM QUALIFICATIONS:

1. Experience in building maintenance operations or comparable position in a service-oriented company. Registered Building Service Manager (RBSM) preferred.

2. Good people skills. Essential

3. Ability to interface with customer personnel. Essential

4. Basic understanding of cost control. Essential

5. Must have a valid driver's license and a good driving record. Essential

PHYSICAL REQUIREMENTS:

Visual acuity to the extent that the person can see dirt on floors, windows improperly cleaned, dust on tables, etc. Hearing/speaking ability in English, and in some cases, another language, to the extent that the person can communicate with employees and prospective employees in person and on the telephone. Hearing/speaking ability to communicate with customers in English. The ability to conduct training classes as well as on-the-job training. Ability to the extent that the person can identify safety hazards such as frayed cords, wet floors, lifting hazards, etc. Some Production Supervisor positions may require cleaning responsibilities. Because demonstration is the preferred method of instruction, and the Production Supervisor is involved in new job starts, the incumbent must be able to lift 40 pounds and perform cleaning duties involving lifting, standing, bending and twisting.

JOB LOCATION:

Headquarters may be in the District Office. Locations and times of work will vary by need in all locations. Travel to all Area / Project locations as needed.

DUTIES:

The Production Supervisor is responsible for directing all *Your Company Name* activities within his or her geographic area in accordance with *Your Company Name* policies and procedures. These include:

1. Coordinates and supervises duties within the area.

2. Controls direct cost.

3. Assigns personnel to accounts. Maintains "relief" (floater) pool.

4. Responsible for customer relations. Visits clients at least monthly. More frequent visits with "top 10" customers - those customers representing the top 10 accounts in terms of margin in the area.

5. Prepares schedules and supervises work assignments for Area Supervisors, Site Supervisors, team crews, and in some District locations, floor and carpet crews.

6. Ensures that the work identified in the specifications is performed properly, on time, safely and within the budget.

7. Uses computer products to track work. These products include: work tickets, project status reports, comparison report, and hours-by-employee report.

8. Conducts training for Area Supervisors, Site Supervisors, team crews, and in some District locations, floor and carpet crews. Ensures that all personnel are properly trained so they can accomplish all assigned duties and work in a safe manner. Maintains training records on all assigned personnel.

9. Orders and delivers cleaning supplies and equipment. Maintains security of all supplies, tools and equipment.

10. Administers the *Your Company Name* Safety program within the area. Investigates any on-the-job accidents or

incidents and prepares appropriate reports. Participates in customer safety meeting if requested.

11. Enforces the account/District dress code.

12. Administers *Your Company Name* personnel policies in accordance with *Your Company Name* personnel policy manual.

13. Maintains quality control over all work performed by assigned personnel through regular Job Status Reports and positive feedback.

14. Prepares required reports.

15. Responds daily to oral requests from customers.

16. Completes all work in a professional manner commensurate with industry and safety standards.

17. Markets expanded/new services to clients within existing accounts. At some District locations, may also have responsibility for outside sales to new prospects and tag sales to current customers.

18. Any other duties as assigned.

MAJOR GOALS:

1. To have a profitable area and to exploit growth opportunities within existing accounts and in new accounts.

2. To deliver the product or service to meet or exceed our customers' needs, expectations and standards.

3. To develop key personnel and strive to ensure their success.

SUBORDINATE GOALS AND KEY RESULTS:

1. To continue to improve customer relations, the Production Supervisor will be successful in this Key Results Area when:

   a. A customer contact schedule is established and adhered to.

   b. Customers are contacted pursuant to the customer contact schedule.

   c. Customers are encouraged to contact him/her when issues arise.

   d. Customer Communication Log Books are established in each account. The books are reviewed daily by the Site/Assistant/Area Supervisor. Any actions are taken promptly and follow up done. Action taken is documented in the Customer Communication Log Book and, if appropriate, verbally with the customer.

   e. Customer complaints and concerns are successfully resolved within the time period agreed upon between the Production Supervisor and the customer.

   f. Each account is inspected by the Production Supervisor during or subsequent to each customer meeting.

2. To develop Supervisors and potential Supervisors, the Production Supervisor will be successful in this Key Results Area when:

   a. All Supervisors have completed the *Your Company Name* Supervisory Course.

b. All Supervisors attend quarterly *Your Company Name* District meetings.

c. Potential Supervisors are identified and afforded the opportunity to complete the *Your Company Name* Supervisory Course.

3. To maintain operational control of the accounts, the Production Supervisor will be successful in this Key Results Area when:

   a. Individual Account Operations Manuals are established and maintained.

   b. Project scheduling is established and maintained in each account.

   c. Job costs are analyzed and planning is implemented to continue to maintain cost in each job at a profitable level.

   d. Schedules of maintenance are maintained for each job.

   e. Inspections and walkthroughs, utilizing the Job Status Reports, continue to ensure that tasks are being completed in a timely, safe and workable manner.

   f. Customer complaints are minimal, and corrected in a timely manner. (For most issues, this means the same day.)

4. To improve internal communications (lateral & vertical), the Production Supervisor will be successful in this Key Results Area when:

   a. Customer complaints are given to and acted upon by Site/Area Supervisors and cleaning specialists within the time period set by the Production Supervisor and corrective action is verified.

b. Immediate Action requests are given to and acted upon by the Site/Area Supervisors and cleaning specialists within the time period set by the Production Supervisor and corrective action verified.

c. An "open door" policy is established and maintained by the Production Supervisor.

d. All issues not within the area of responsibility of the Production Supervisor which come to his/her attention are given immediately to the individual responsible.

e. A chain of command is established in order to ensure that Site Supervisors not only report to the Production Supervisor, but respond correctly to communications with the customer.

f. All changes in the Schedule Of Maintenance or procedures are reduced to writing and submitted to the *Your Company Name* Corporate Office, and that the newly produced data is given to the customer, and to the Account Operations Manual within five working days of the change.

g. A smooth, cooperative working relationship exists with other departments within *Your Company Name*.

5. To develop management skills through active participation in development opportunities, the Production Supervisor will be successful in this Key Results Area when:

a. He/she has completed the RBSM course of study.

b. He/she has received the RBSM Certification.

c. He/she reflects a positive image of themselves and the Company.

6. To improve employee job satisfaction, the Production Supervisor will be successful in this Key Results Area when:

   a. He/she properly ensures that each employee receives an accurate and timely error-free paycheck on the scheduled pay date, i.e. no hand checks.

   b. Turnover and absenteeism are minimal.

   c. He/she, weekly, seeks out and compliments at least one employee for a job well done.

7. To explore growth opportunities, the Production Supervisor will be successful in this Key Results Area when:

   a. New service or expansion of current services and/ or Tag jobs have been identified and suggested to customers.

   b. During the year, one new service has been added to the area.

8. To create a safe work place, the Production Supervisor will be successful in this Key Results Area when:

   a. All subordinate Supervisors actively support the safety program and enforce the provisions.

   b. Material Safety Data Sheets (MSDS) are on hand in each account and are current.

   c. All employees receive the required training.

d. All employees use the required safety equipment.

e. Safety is a factor in considering equipment or chemical purchase recommendations.

f. Accidents are promptly reported and investigated in accordance with District and Company policy.

g. Accident investigation reports include practical steps to prevent reoccurrence.

h. Products are properly labeled.

i. Safety meetings are held at each job site per prearranged schedule.

9. To properly administer personnel policies, the Production Supervisor will have been successful in this Key Results Area when:

a. Employee grievances are at a minimum.

b. No complaints are filed with city, county, state, or federal Equal Employment Opportunity Commission (EEOC) offices. (And if complaints are filed, *Your Company Name* prevails in subsequent judgments.)

c. Disciplinary actions are timely, proper and documented in accordance with Company policy.

d. Interviewing and hiring actions are proper.

(1) I-9 forms are properly completed.

(2) Hiring documents are completed and distributed to the District office on a timely basis.

e. Equal Employment Opportunity (EEO) and Affirmative Action policies are implemented.

ORGANIZATIONAL RELATIONSHIPS:

The Production Supervisor is supervised by the District Manager for assignment, guidance, evaluation and problem solving. Since there is daily telephone and in-person contact with internal and external customers, a harmonious and cooperative attitude must be maintained.

NOTE:

Job/Position Descriptions are written to give employees and supervisors information about the job. They are not contracts of any kind. Employees can be reassigned at any time and given other duties within the corporation. Not all jobs have position descriptions. It is impossible to list each and every duty in a position description. Other duties may be assigned.

Your Company Name
Staff Position Description and Specifications
Revised Effective _____

Area Supervisor   Page __ of __

POSITION TITLE: Area Supervisor

REPORTS TO: Production Supervisor/Project or District Manager. Also responds to requests/instructions from the customer.

DEFINITION:

1. The Area Supervisor's duties differ considerably by Area or District location. In some District locations, the Area Supervisor will interview and hire the crew.

2. The Area Supervisor is a part-time or full-time person responsible for assisting a Production Supervisor or District Manager with supervision of several accounts.

3. The Area Supervisor is responsible for ensuring that the accounts are cleaned according to contract specifications. He or she supervises the cleaning crews.

4. Depending upon District location, he or she conducts the orientation and training, counsels and disciplines subordinates; orders and delivers supplies and sends equipment for repair (or repairs on site) as needed.

5. May be subject to 24-hour on-call responsibilities.

MINIMUM QUALIFICATIONS:

1. Experience in building maintenance operations.

2. Prefer experience in supervising people in any capacity.

3. Good people skills.

4. Ability to interface with customer personnel is essential.

5. Customer relations may be a part of the Area Supervisor's position depending upon the schedule.

6. Should be a graduate of the *Your Company Name* Supervisor's Training Program.

7. Must have valid driver's license and good driving record.

PHYSICAL REQUIREMENTS:

Must be able to lift 50 pounds and perform routine physical activity associated with carpet and hard surface floor care. Must be able to stand and walk for long periods of time. Extended and repeated twisting and stooping required. Visual acuity to the extent that the person can see stains on carpets, dust on surfaces, trash or small items on the floor, etc., is required.

Hearing/speaking ability in English and in some cases, another language, to the extent that the person can communicate with employees in person and on the phone. Hearing/speaking ability to communicate with customers in English.

JOB LOCATION:

Headquarters may be in the District/Project Office. Locations and times of work will vary by need in all locations. Travel to all Area/Project locations as needed.

DUTIES:

1. Maintains and delivers supplies and equipment. Keeps track of cleaning chemicals and supplies used and ensures that sufficient items are on hand to properly clean the building.

2. Safeguards and is accountable for all equipment, tools and supplies.

3. Inspects janitorial closets for compliance with safety standards.

4. Fills in for absent cleaners.

5. Performs special tasks such as stripping and refinishing floors, carpet care, etc.

6. Administers *Your Company Name* personnel policies in accordance with *Your Company Name* personnel policy manual.

7. Enforces the account/District dress code.

8. Assists in training new Supervisors/Lead People.

9. Maintains equipment. Picks up equipment needing repair, brings it to the office and returns it to the account when repaired. May also repair equipment.

10. Other duties as required.

MAJOR GOAL:

To assist the Production Supervisor/District Manager in ensuring that all tasks identified in the specifications are performed on time, safely, properly and within budget.

SUBORDINATE GOALS AND KEY RESULTS:

1. To train personnel and to increase personal professionalism in this industry, the Area Supervisor will be successful in this Key Results Area when:

   a. He/she has designated one person as an Area Supervisor trainee and begun training.

b. He/she has trained all Site Supervisors/Assistant Site Supervisors to be effective Supervisors.

c. Site Supervisors/Assistant Site Supervisors in the area attend quarterly Supervisor's meetings.

d. He/she has attended Quarterly Supervisors' Meetings.

e. He/she has reviewed at least one training video tape each quarter.

f. He/she has learned one new skill during each quarter.

g. He/she has learned the tasks performed in the accounts and is able to do them without supervision.

2. To plan ahead so that supplies and equipment are always on hand, the Area Supervisor will be successful in this Key Results Area when:

a. Employees inventory their supply needs at the end of each shift and report any shortages to Site Supervisors.

b. Area Supervisors order supplies at least 3 days in advance so that the supply can be delivered with adequate lead time.

c. Defective equipment is promptly repaired.

3. To create a safe work place, the Area Supervisor will be successful in this Key Results Area when:

a. Material Safety Data Sheets (MSDS) are current and personnel trained on them.

b. Personnel use required safety equipment.

c. Employees know the proper use of chemicals.

d. Site Supervisors or Assistant Site Supervisors conduct safety briefings at the beginning or end of each shift or during breaks.

e. Supervisors/Assistant Site Supervisors and employees participate in safety programs.

f. Any accidents or incidents are promptly reported and investigated in accordance with District/Company policies.

g. Products are properly labeled.

4. To properly administer personnel policies, the Area Supervisor will have been successful in this Key Results Area when:

a. Employee grievances are at a minimum.

b. No complaints are filed with city, county, state or federal Equal Employment Opportunity Commission (EEOC) offices. (And, if complaints are filed, *Your Company Name* prevails in subsequent judgments.)

c. Disciplinary actions are timely, proper and documented in accordance with Company policies.

5. To effectively control the work so that it is done properly and safely, the Area Supervisor will be successful in this Key Results Area when:

a. Time is set aside for inspection of the work.

b. The Accounts Operations Manual is up to date.

c. The Customer Communications Log is read nightly, acted upon, and corrective action followed up on and documented.

d. Customer complaints are minimal.

e. The job is done in accordance with specifications.

f. The job is done within the budgeted hours.

6. To improve internal communications, the Area Supervisor will be successful in this Key Results Area when:

a. All Supervisors/Assistant Site Supervisors and employees are aware of *Your Company Name* policies and specific policies in the account.

b. All Supervisors/Assistant Site Supervisors and employees are aware of Job Status Reports and customer complaints as well as customer compliments.

7. To improve employee job satisfaction, the Area Supervisor will be successful in this Key Results Area when:

a. He/she properly insures that each employee receives an accurate and timely error-free paycheck on the scheduled pay date, i.e. no hand checks.

b. Absenteeism is kept to a minimum.

c. Turnover is kept to a minimum.

d. He/she, daily, seeks out and compliments at least one employee for a job well done.

ORGANIZATIONAL RELATIONSHIPS:

The Area Supervisor is supervised by the Production Supervisor/ District Manager or Project Manager for assignments, guidance, evaluation and problem solving. Since there is daily telephone and in-person contact with internal and external customers, a harmonious and cooperative attitude must be maintained.

NOTE:

Job/Position Descriptions are written to give employees and supervisors information about the job. They are not contracts of any kind. Employees can be reassigned at any time and given other duties within the corporation. Not all jobs have position descriptions. It is impossible to list each and every duty in a position description and employees are expected to follow the instructions of their supervisor whether or not those instructions are included in a job description.

Your Company Name
Staff Position Description and Specifications
Revised Effective _____

Assistant Site Supervisor/   Page __ of __
Team Leader

POSITION TITLE: Assistant Site Supervisor/Team Leader
REPORTS TO: Site/Production Supervisor and Project/
                  District Manager. Also responds to requests /
                  instructions from the customer.

DEFINITION:

1. The Assistant Site Supervisor/Team Leader's duties differ considerably by Area or District location. In some District locations, the Assistant Site Supervisor/Team Leader will interview and hire the crew.

2. An Assistant Site Supervisor/Team Leader is a part-time or full-time person responsible for assisting a Production Supervisor or District Manager with supervision of several accounts.

3. The Assistant Site Supervisor/Team Leader is responsible for ensuring that the accounts are cleaned according to contract specifications. He or she supervises the cleaning crews.

4. Depending upon District location, he or she conducts the orientation to the building for employees, trains new people, counsels and disciplines subordinates; orders and delivers supplies and sends equipment for repair (or repairs on site) as needed.

5. May be subject to 24-hour on-call responsibilities.

MINIMUM QUALIFICATIONS:

1. Experience in building maintenance operations.

2. Prefer experience in supervising people in any capacity.

3. Good people skills.

4. Ability to interface with customer personnel is essential.

5. Customer relations may be a part of the Assistant Site Supervisor/Team Leader's position depending upon the schedule.

6. Should be a graduate of the *Your Company Name* Supervisor's Training Program.

7. Must have valid driver's license and good driving record.

PHYSICAL REQUIREMENTS:

Must be able to lift 50 pounds and perform routine physical activity associated with carpet and hard surface floor care. Must be able to stand and walk for long periods of time. Extended and repeated twisting and stooping required. Visual acuity to the extent that the person can see stains on carpets, dust on surfaces, trash or small items on the floor, etc., is required.

Hearing/speaking ability in English and in some cases, another language, to the extent that the person can communicate with employees in person and on the phone. Hearing/speaking ability to communicate with customers in English.

JOB LOCATION:

Headquarters may be in the District/Project/Site Office. Locations and times of work will vary by need in all locations. Travel to all Area/Project locations as needed.

DUTIES:

1. Maintains and delivers supplies and equipment. Keeps track of cleaning chemicals and supplies used and ensures that sufficient items are on hand to properly clean the building.

2. Safeguards and is accountable for all equipment, tools and supplies.

3. Inspects janitorial closets for compliance with safety standards.

4. Fills in for absent cleaners.

5. Performs special tasks such as stripping and refinishing floors, carpet care, etc.

6. Administers *Your Company Name* personnel policies in accordance with *Your Company Name* personnel policy manual.

7. Enforces the account/District dress code.

8. Assists in training new Supervisors.

9. Maintains equipment. Picks up equipment needing repair, brings it to the office and returns it to the account when repaired. May also repair equipment.

10. Other duties as required.

MAJOR GOAL:

To assist the Site Supervisor, Production Supervisor and District Manager in ensuring that all tasks identified in the specifications are performed on time, safely, properly and within budget.

SUBORDINATE GOALS AND KEY RESULTS:

1. To train personnel and to increase personal professionalism in this industry, the Assistant Site Supervisor/Team Leader will be successful in this Key Results Area when:

   a. He/she has designated one person as an Assistant Site Supervisor/Team Leader trainee and begun training.

   b. He/she has trained all Cleaning Specialists to be effective Supervisors.

   c. He/she has attended Quarterly Supervisors' Meetings.

   d. He/she has reviewed at least one training video tape each quarter.

   e. He/she has learned one new skill during each quarter.

   f. He/she has learned the tasks performed in the accounts and is able to do them without supervision.

2. To plan ahead so that supplies and equipment are always on hand, the Assistant Site Supervisor/Team Leader will be successful in this Key Results Area when:

   a. The Assistant Site Supervisor/Team Leader orders supplies at least 3 days in advance so that the supply can be delivered with adequate lead time.

   b. Defective equipment is promptly repaired.

3. To create a safe work place, the Assistant Site Supervisor/Team Leader will be successful in this Key Results Area when:

   a. Material Safety Data Sheets (MSDS) are current and personnel trained on them.

   b. Personnel use required safety equipment.

   c. Employees know the proper use of chemicals.

   d. He/she conducts safety briefings at the beginning or end of each shift or during breaks.

   e. All team employees participate in safety programs.

   f. Any accidents or incidents are promptly reported and investigated in accordance with District/Company policies.

   g. Products are properly labeled.

4. To properly administer personnel policies, the Assistant Site Supervisor/Team Leader will have been successful in this Key Results Area when:

   a. Employee grievances are at a minimum.

   b. No complaints are filed with city, county, state or federal Equal Employment Opportunity Commission (EEOC) offices. (And, if complaints are filed, *Your Company Name* prevails in subsequent judgments.)

   c. Disciplinary actions are timely, proper and documented in accordance with Company policies.

5.   To effectively control the work so that it is done properly and safely, the Assistant Site Supervisor/ Team Leader will be successful in this Key Results Area when:

   a. Time is set aside for inspection of the work.

   b. The Accounts Operations Manual is up to date.

   c. The Customer Communications Log is read nightly, acted upon, and corrective action followed up on and documented.

   d. Customer complaints are minimal.

   e. The job is done in accordance with specifications.

   f. The job is done within the budgeted hours.

6.   To improve internal communications, the Assistant Site Supervisor/Team Leader will be successful in this Key Results Area when:

   a. All team employees are aware of *Your Company Name* policies and specific policies in the account.

   b. All employees are aware of Job Status Reports and customer complaints as well as customer compliments.

7.   To improve employee job satisfaction, the Assistant Site Supervisor/Team Leader will be successful in this Key Results Area when:

   a. He/she properly insures that each employee receives an accurate and timely error-free paycheck on the scheduled pay date, i.e. no hand checks.

b. Absenteeism is kept to a minimum.

c. Turnover is kept to a minimum.

d. He/she, daily, seeks out and compliments at least one employee for a job well done.

ORGANIZATIONAL RELATIONSHIPS:

The Assistant Site Supervisor/Team Leader is supervised by the Site Supervisor, Production Supervisor, District Manager or Project Manager for assignments, guidance, evaluation and problem solving. Since there is daily telephone and in-person contact with internal and external customers, a harmonious and cooperative attitude must be maintained.

NOTE:

Job/Position Descriptions are written to give employees and supervisors information about the job. They are not contracts of any kind. Employees can be reassigned at any time and given other duties within the corporation. Not all jobs have position descriptions. It is impossible to list each and every duty in a position description and employees are expected to follow the instructions of their supervisor whether or not those instructions are included in a job description.

Your Company Name
Staff Position Description and Specifications
Revised Effective _____

Site Supervisor   Page ___ of ___

POSITION TITLE: Site Supervisor
REPORTS TO: District Manager, Operations Manager, Production Supervisor or Area Supervisor. Also responds to requests/instructions from the customer.

DEFINITION:

1. A Site Supervisor is a full- or part-time person responsible for all custodial tasks within one account. A Site Supervisor may supervise one large account within the District location or a small geographically separated unit.

2. In some District locations, the Site Supervisor may interview and hire the crew. In all locations, the Site Supervisor is responsible for training and supervision.

3. The Site Supervisor also interfaces with the customer to ensure customer satisfaction with our work.

4. The overall goal and first priority of the Site Supervisor is to become an important resource for the customer. He or she is to have the best interests of the customer in mind in all scheduling decisions.

MINIMUM QUALIFICATIONS:

1. Experience in building maintenance operations.

2. Prefer experience managing large cleaning crew.

3. Good people skills.

4. Ability to interface with customer personnel essential.

5. Must have valid driver's license and good driving record.

PHYSICAL REQUIREMENTS:

Must be able to lift 50 pounds and perform routine physical activity associated with dusting, trashing, and operating equipment such as a vacuum cleaner. Must be able to stand and walk for long periods of time. Extensive repeated twisting and stooping required. Visual acuity to the extent that the person can see stains on carpets, dust on surfaces, trash or small items on the floor, etc., is required.

JOB LOCATION:

Headquarters will be the site location of the job. Locations and time of work will vary by need in all locations. Travel to District/ Project Office as needed.

DUTIES:

1. Ensures that the work identified in the specifications is performed properly, on time, safely and within the budget.

2. Schedules and coordinates custodial duties with the customer. Prepares schedule and supervises work assignments for all personnel.

3. Inspects work of subordinates.

4. Ensures the Account Operations Manual is up to date and procedures are followed.

5. Conducts training for *Your Company Name* employees.

6. Orders all cleaning supplies and equipment. Maintains security of all supplies, tools and equipment.

7. Enforces the account/District dress code.

8. Administers *Your Company Name* personnel policies in accordance with *Your Company Name* personnel policy manual.

9. Administers the *Your Company Name* Safety Program at the account.

10. Prepares required reports.

11. Performs cleaning duties.

12. Responds daily to oral requests from the customer.

13. Completes all work in a professional manner commensurate with industry and safety standards.

14. Any other duties as assigned.

MAJOR GOAL:

To achieve required margins; to satisfy the customer; and, to explore and exploit growth opportunities within the account.

SUBORDINATE GOALS AND KEY RESULTS:

1. To maintain effective customer relations, the Site Supervisor will be successful in this Key Results Area when:

   a. A contact schedule is established with major tenants/ executives and the schedule is followed. (Applicable if tenant contact is encouraged.)

   b. The client is encouraged to contact him/her when issues arise.

c. The Customer Communications Log Book is read nightly, acted upon, and corrective action followed up on and documented.

d. Customer complaints and concerns are successfully resolved within the time period agreed upon.

e. The Immediate Attention Form is given to and acted upon by responsible person or persons.

f. All changes in account cleaning specifications or procedures are reduced to writing with copies to the Corporate Office and the client within five working days of the change.

2. To develop Supervisors and potential Supervisors, the Site Supervisor will be successful in this Key Results Area when:

a. Cleaners have been trained on their assigned duties.

b. All current Supervisors/Team Leaders have been trained.

c. All employees attend monthly meetings.

d. Potential Supervisors have been identified and are afforded the opportunity to complete the *Your Company Name* Supervisory Development Course.

3. To maintain operational control of the account, the Site Supervisor will be successful in this Key Results Area when:

a. The Account Operations Manual is maintained and procedures followed.

b. The Account Operations Manual is up to date.

    c.   Project Scheduling is established and maintained.

    d.   Job costs are analyzed and planning is implemented to continue to maintain costs at or below budget. (NOTE: Operating below budget within specifications. Any changes in the specifications, products used, or service must be approved in advance.)

    e.   Inspections and walkthroughs continue to insure that tasks are being completed in a timely, safe and workmanlike manner.

4. To develop management skills through active participation in development opportunities, the Site Supervisor will be successful in this Key Results Area when:

    a.   The Site Supervisor completes the training outlined in the *Your Company Name* Supervisor Training Course.

5. To improve employee job satisfactions, the Site Supervisor will be successful in this Key Results Area when:

    a.   He/she properly ensures that each employee receives an accurate and timely error-free paycheck on the scheduled pay date, i.e. no hand checks.

    b.   Absenteeism and turnover are minimal.

    c.   The Site Supervisor weekly seeks out and compliments at least one employee for a job well done.

6. To explore growth opportunities, the Site Supervisor will be successful in this Key Results Area when:

a. Opportunities for additional services have been identified and communicated to the District/Project/Operations Manager and/or the Production Supervisor.

b. Tag work is sold to the customer.

7. To create a safe work place, the Site Supervisor will be successful in this Key Results Area when:

   a. All subordinate Supervisors actively support the safety program and enforce the provisions.

   b. Material Safety Data Sheets (MSDS) are on hand and are current.

   c. All employees receive the required training and documentation.

   d. All employees use the required safety equipment.

   e. Safety is a factor in considering equipment or chemical purchases.

   f. Accidents are promptly reported and investigated in accordance with Company/District policies.

   g. Accident investigation reports include practical steps to prevent reoccurrence.

   h. Products are properly labeled.

8. To properly administer personnel policies, the Site Supervisor will have been successful in this Key Results Area when:

   a. Employee grievances are at a minimum.

   b. No complaints are filed with city, county, state or federal Equal Employment Opportunity Commission

(EEOC) offices. (And, if complaints are filed, *Your Company Name* prevails in subsequent judgments.)

c. Discipline is timely, proper and documented in accordance with Company policy.

d. If interviewing and hiring is done on Site:

(1) I-9 forms are properly completed.

(2) Police checks are properly conducted.

(3) Other paperwork is properly completed.

ORGANIZATIONAL RELATIONSHIPS:

The Site Supervisor is supervised by the Area, District, and Operations Manager or Project Manager for assignments, guidance, evaluation and problem solving. Since there is daily telephone and in-person contact with internal and external customers, a harmonious and cooperative attitude must be maintained.

NOTE:

Job/Position Descriptions are written to give employees and Supervisors information about the job. They are not contracts of any kind. Employees can be reassigned at any time and given other duties within the Corporation. Not all jobs have position descriptions. It is impossible to list each and every duty in a position description and employees are expected to follow the instructions of their Supervisor whether or not those instructions are included in a job description.

Your Company Name
Staff Position Description and Specifications
Revised Effective _____
District Administrative Assistant   Page __ of __

POSITION TITLE: District Administrative Assistant

REPORTS TO: District Manager

DEFINITION:

The District Administrative Assistant assists the District Manager in a variety of administrative, accounting, sales, customer relations and human resources areas.

MINIMUM QUALIFICATIONS:

1. Experience with a popular word processing program required. Microsoft Word for Windows preferred.

2. Ability to communicate in English, both oral and written, required.

3. Ability to communicate orally in Spanish may be required.

4. Bookkeeping experience helpful.

5. Ability to effectively deal with short suspense requirements and multiple priorities essential.

6. Ability to effectively deal with customers, employees, potential employees, and regulating government representatives essential.

7. Valid driver's license and good driving record.

PHYSICAL REQUIREMENTS:

Visual acuity to the extent that the person can use a PC for creating, editing and proof reading word processing documents, and input data in to the TEAM Financial Management System. Hearing/speaking ability in English to the extent that the person can answer the telephone, take messages, refer callers to the correct person, etc.

JOB LOCATION: District Office

DUTIES:

The District Administrative Assistant is responsible for assisting the District Manager and staff in all *Your Company Name* activities within the District in accordance with *Your Company Name* policies and procedures. These include:

1. Recruitment.

2. Human Resources.

3. Office Administration.

4. Operations.

5. Accounting.

6. Marketing.

7. Customer Relations.

8. Safety.

9. Training and evaluation.

10. Supply.

MAJOR GOAL:

To assist the District Manager and staff to maintain a profitable District and meet District profit margin and growth goals.

SUBORDINATE GOAL AND KEY RESULTS:

1. To maintain an effective recruitment program, the District Administrative Assistant will be successful in this Key Results Area when:

    a. Help wanted advertising is timely and cost effective.

    b. All District positions are filled.

2. To maintain an effective human resources program, the District Administrative Assistant will be successful in this Key Results Area when:

    a. New hires are screened in accordance with *Your Company Name* policy, i.e., screening and police records checks.

    b. Personnel files are orderly and proper.

    c. Disciplinary actions, including terminations, are proper. If disciplinary actions are challenged in court or by an administrative hearing, *Your Company Name* prevails.

    d. Unemployment compensation is minimized and *Your Company Name* prevails in Unemployment Compensation hearings.

    e. Recognition programs, Team of the Month, Employee of the Year, are established and ongoing. Employee recognition is publicized in company newsletter.

f. Orientation class is conducted for new hires.

g. Prospective employee data base is maintained.

h. He/she ensures that each employee receives an accurate and timely error-free paycheck on the scheduled pay date, i.e. no hand checks.

i. Attend the ongoing Supervisor's training program. Minimum requirement is Quarterly Supervisor's meetings.

j. Uniform inventory is maintained and available for issue.

3. To maintain efficient office administration, the District Administrative Assistant will be successful in this Key Results Area when:

a. Files are orderly.

b. Correspondence is timely.

c. Records are properly maintained.

d. All necessary *Your Company Name* forms are on hand and easy to locate.

e. Telephone messages are communicated promptly.

f. Customers calling about complaints are reassured that action will be taken.

g. Customer complaints taken over the phone are immediately referred to the proper Manager/ Supervisor.

4. To ensure timely and effective administrative, accounting and clerical assistance to the operations staff, the District

Administrative Assistant will be successful in this Key Results Area when:

a. TEAM Financial Management reports are distributed to the Managers so that they can comply with the management information requirements of the Operations Manual.

b. Procedures outlined in the Administrative Manual are followed.

c. Clerical assistance to the operations staff is timely. This assistance includes typing inspection reports, lesson plans, job descriptions, etc.

d. Account Operations Manuals are prepared for the staff as needed.

e. Vehicle Logs and assignments are maintained.

5. To ensure that District accounting practices are proper, reports are timely and accurate, the District Administrative Assistant will be successful in this Key Results when:

a. Timekeeping errors are under 1%.

b. Prompt adjustments to timekeeping reports are made.

c. Reports to the Corporate Office are on time and accurate.

d. District accounting practices are in compliance with the *Your Company Name* District Procedures Manual.

6. To ensure that Administrative Assistance to the marketing program is timely and effective, the District

Administrative Assistant will be successful in this Key Results Area when:

    a. He/she maintains a suspense file on sales leads provided from Corporate telemarketing and from District efforts.

7. To ensure that the District Administrative Assistant participates in customer relations programs, he/she will be successful in this Key Results Area when:

    a. He/she maintains a calendar of Job Status calls and reacts to customer needs.

8. To ensure that the District Administrative Assistant assists in the District Safety Program, he/she will be successful in this Key Results Area when:

    a. A book of Material Safety Data Sheets (MSDS) used in the District is maintained.

    b. Monthly safety meetings are held.

    c. Accident/incident reports are forwarded to the Corporate Office, the state and the insurance company as required by the *Your Company Name* Safety Manual.

9. To ensure that training aids are on hand for entry level, Supervisor and Manager training, the District Administrative Assistant will be successful in this Key Results Area when:

    a. *Your Company Name* Lesson Plans are available in the District Office.

    b. Video tapes are available for in-office and checkout use.

    c. The Building Service Contractor's International (BSCAI) Independent Study Guide is available for use.

    d. Other BSCAI materials, including the Carpet Care and Hard Surface Care Manuals are on hand.

10. To ensure that supply procedures are timely and proper, the District Administrative Assistant will be successful in this Key Results Area when:

    a. Managers have the supplies and equipment that they need while the on-hand inventory is limited. (This requires using the supplier as the warehouse.)

    b. Purchase orders are prepared in accordance with *Your Company Name* procedures. Opportunities for resale are exploited.

ORGANIZATIONAL RELATIONSHIPS:

The District Administrative Assistant is supervised by the District Manager for assignment, guidance, evaluation and problem solving. Since there is daily telephone and in-person contact with internal and external customers, a harmonious and cooperative attitude must be maintained.

NOTE:

Job/Position Descriptions are written to give employees and Supervisors information about the job. They are not contracts of any kind. Employees can be reassigned at any time and given other duties within the Corporation. Not all jobs have position descriptions. It is impossible to list each and every duty in a position description and employees are expected to follow the instructions of their Supervisor whether or not those instructions are included in a job description.

Your Company Name
Staff Position Description and Specifications
Revised Effective _____

District Trainer   Page __ of __

POSITION TITLE: District Trainer

REPORTS TO: District Manager

DEFINITION:

The District Trainer is responsible for managing all the training activity within a District.

1. In some locations he or she may actually conduct training, while in others he or she ensures that the training conducted by others is timely and effective.

2. In most, if not all, locations the training responsibilities are an additional duty assigned to a full-time person in the District.

3. Since many of the District Trainer's goals and Key Results Areas are achieved through the efforts of others, he or she must be a person who can influence and motivate others to achieve these results.

MINIMUM QUALIFICATIONS:

1. Experience in cleaning operations, including hard floor and carpet care.

2. Experience as a Supervisor of a cleaning operation preferred.

3. Training experience preferred.

PHYSICAL REQUIREMENTS:

Requires visual acuity to the extent that the District Trainer can easily see soil and stains, dust, etc., so that he or she can inspect the work of students. Hearing/speaking ability in English and, in some cases, another language, to the extent that the incumbent can communicate orally over the telephone with staff and face to face with students and staff. Because demonstration is the preferred method of instruction, the District Trainer must be able to lift 40 pounds and perform cleaning duties involving lifting, standing, bending and twisting.

JOB LOCATION:

Locations and times of work will vary by District.

DUTIES:

1. Schedules and/or conducts orientation program for new hires.

2. Schedules and participates in Quarterly Supervisors' Meetings.

3. Conducts and/or assists in Supervisors' training.

4. Ensures availability of *Your Company Name,* Building Service Contractor's Association International (BSCAI) and other training materials.

5. Ensures availability of position results descriptions.

6. Other duties as required.

MAJOR GOAL:

To ensure that all District personnel are capable of performing their duties professionally and safely in accordance with *Your Company Name,* industry and safety standards.

SUBORDINATE GOALS AND KEY RESULTS:

1. To ensure that all new hires receive orientation training, the District Trainer will be successful in this Key Results Area when:

   a. All new hires undergo an orientation program in accordance with *Your Company Name* lesson plans.

   b. All new hires receive safety training during orientation.

   c. All training documentation is current and complete.

2. To ensure that all new hires receive basic skills training either in the office or on-site, the District Trainer will be successful in this Key Results Area when:

   a. All new hires are trained in basic skills for general office and restroom cleaning.

   b. Training is conducted in the District Office or on-site.

   c. Training is conducted in accordance with *Your Company Name* lesson plans.

3. To ensure that Supervisors and cleaners are technically competent, the District Trainer will be successful in this Key Results Area when:

   a. Personnel responsible for hard surface floor care have been trained in accordance with *Your Company Name* lesson plans and BSCAI videos.

   b. Personnel responsible for carpet care have been trained in accordance with *Your Company Name* lesson plans and BSCAI videos.

   c. Customer claims for damage caused by improper use of chemicals or poor techniques have been eliminated.

   d. Expensive redo's caused by improper use of chemicals or poor techniques have been eliminated.

   e. Stripping and refinishing floors are done no more frequently than required by specifications, and are not caused by improper floor care techniques.

   f. Extraction is done no more frequently than required by specifications.

   g. Accounts are not running over hours because cleaners aren't properly trained.

4. To ensure that cleaners have position descriptions, the District Trainer will be successful in this Key Results Area when:

   a. Position descriptions for cleaners are available in the account operations manual.

   b. Personnel know their duties as identified in the position description.

5. To ensure that a staff of personnel capable of becoming Site/Area Supervisors is maintained and trained, the District Trainer will be successful in this Key Results Area when:

   a. He or she identifies potential Supervisor trainees to the District Manager.

   b. He or she conducts periodic Supervisor training using *Your Company Name* lesson plans and training programs sponsored by approved chemical and equipment vendors.

6. To ensure that *Your Company Name*, BSCAI and other training materials are available to District personnel, the District Trainer will be successful in this Key Results Area when:

   a. *Your Company Name* lesson plans are in place in the District Office and in all accounts with a full-time Production Supervisor or Project Manager.

   b. BSCAI Self-Study Materials are available for checkout in the District Office.

   c. A library of video tape material is maintained for self-study.

7. To ensure that monthly Supervisor's meetings are held, the District Trainer will be successful in this Key Results Area when:

   a. Site Supervisors, Area Supervisors and District management attend quarterly Supervisors' meetings.

   b. At least one technical topic is covered during each meeting using *Your Company Name* lesson plans, BSCAI videotapes and/or training programs sponsored by chemical or equipment vendors.

   c. Safety is covered in every Supervisor's meeting.

8. To ensure that all Supervisors and Managers have up-to-date position results descriptions, the District Trainer will be successful in this Key Results Area when:

   a. A complete set of basic position descriptions is available in the office.

    b. Position descriptions for Supervisors and Managers have been tailored to the District and account requirements.

9. To ensure that Managers participate in professional training and certification, the District Trainer will be successful in this Key Results Area when:

    a. Production Supervisors, Area and Site Supervisors study for RBSM.

    b. District Managers study for the CBSE.

10. To ensure that all District personnel are trained in their safety responsibilities, the District Trainer will be successful in this Key Results Area when:

    a. Cleaners and Supervisors know what Material Safety Data Sheets are and know where to find them.

    b. Cleaners and Supervisors know the importance of proper labeling.

    c. Supervisors know the importance of stressing safety.

    d. Accident and incident investigations are thorough and that they identify root causes of accidents/incidents.

ORGANIZATIONAL RELATIONSHIPS:

The District Trainer is supervised by the District Manager or Project Manager for assignments, guidance, evaluation and problem solving. Since there is daily telephone and in-person contact with internal and external customers, a harmonious and cooperative attitude must be maintained.

NOTE:

Job/Position Descriptions are written to give employees and Supervisors information about the job. They are not contracts of any kind. Employees can be reassigned at any time and given other duties within the Corporation. Not all jobs have position descriptions. It is impossible to list each and every duty in a position description and employees are expected to follow the instructions of their Supervisor whether or not those instructions are included in a job description.

POSITION TITLE: District Safety Coordinator

REPORTS TO: District Manager

DEFINITION:

1. The District Safety Coordinator is responsible for managing all the safety activity within the District.

2. Except for the *Your Company Name* Corporate Safety Coordinator, District/Project Safety Coordinator responsibilities are additional duties.

3. Since many of the District Safety Coordinator's goals and Key Results Areas are achieved through the efforts of others he or she must be a person who can influence and motivate others to achieve these results.

MINIMUM QUALIFICATIONS:

1. Familiar with Occupational Safety Health Administration (OSHA) and Mine Safety Health Administration (MSHA) safety rules and regulations.

2. Valid driver's license and good driving record.

3. Spreadsheet and word processing experience mandatory.

4. Basic knowledge of worker's compensation rules including calculation of the Modification Factor.

PHYSICAL REQUIREMENTS:

Visual acuity to the extent that the person can identify safety hazards such as frayed cords, wet floors, etc. Hearing/speaking ability in English and, in some cases, another language, to the extent that the Safety Coordinator can interview cleaning personnel about work conditions. Ability to converse over the telephone with District Managers, OSHA personnel, insurance company representatives, etc.

JOB LOCATION:

Locations and times of work will vary by District.

DUTIES:

1. Prepares District Safety policies.

2. Ensures that District personnel are aware of *Your Company Name* and District Safety policies.

3. Conducts safety audits of selected accounts.

4. Schedules and organizes monthly District Safety meetings.

5. Participates in Quarterly Supervisor's Meetings.

6. Recommends policies and procedures to the *Your Company Name* Corporate Safety Coordinator.

7. Other duties as required.

MAJOR GOAL:

To ensure that all District personnel perform their duties safely so as to achieve a zero lost time injury record and zero property and liability claims/losses within the District.

SUBORDINATE GOAL AND KEY RESULTS:

1. To ensure that all personnel are trained in their safety responsibilities, the District Safety Coordinator will be successful in this Key Results Areas when:

    a. All new hires receive safety training during orientation.

    b. Supervisors receive safety training during quarterly Supervisors' meetings.

    c. Managers discuss safety issues during operation meetings.

2. To ensure District compliance with the Right to Know Act, the District Safety Coordinator will be successful in this Key Results Area when:

    a. All personnel know what MSDS sheets are and where to find them.

    b. All personnel have acknowledged training on MSDS and that acknowledgment has been placed in their personnel folders.

    c. MSDS's are current in each account and in the District Office.

    d. All products are properly labeled in all accounts.

3. To ensure that District personnel use appropriate safety equipment, the District Safety Coordinator will be successful in this Key Results Areas when:

    a. Personnel in the accounts use gloves, goggles, safety glasses and other personal protective equipment required by product labels, MSDS's or District policy.

b. Personnel stripping and refinishing floors have been issued personal safety equipment including overshoes and knee protectors.

c. Personnel doing heavy lifting have been issued lifting belts.

4. To implement and monitor a vehicle safety program, the District Safety Coordinator will be successful in this Key Results Area when:

a. All personnel in *Your Company Name* vehicles or in personal vehicles used for *Your Company Name* business use seat belts.

b. All *Your Company Name* vehicles must have Alert decals and Safe Driver stickers.

c. Vehicles are regularly inspected for defects.

5. To ensure that personnel policies and programs support the safety goals, the District Safety Coordinator will be successful in this Key Results Area when:

a. All new hires that drive are screened.

b. Driving records are screened before a person is assigned driving duties.

c. Everyone is briefed on the Drug Free Work place policy and that acknowledgment is placed in their personnel folders.

d. Non-work related injuries are noted in the personnel files.

6. To implement safety motivational and promotion programs, the District Safety Coordinator will be successful in this Key Results Area when:

a. Each job site conducts a safety meeting.

b. Supervisors participate in the monthly District Safety meeting.

c. Safety is discussed at each Supervisor's meeting.

7. To ensure that accident/incidents are investigated promptly and thoroughly, the District Safety Coordinator will be successful in this Key Results Area when:

a. Accident/incident reports are faxed to the *Your Company Name* Corporate Safety Coordinator and *Your Company Name's* insurance agent within 24 hours of the incident.

b. Investigation reports identify the root cause of the incident.

c. Investigation reports cite corrective action to prevent reoccurrence.

8. To ensure that injured workers are returned to duty as soon as practical, the District Safety Coordinator will be successful in this Key Results Area when:

a. A light duty program has been implemented in the District.

b. Someone in the District is designated to maintain contact with injured workers.

c. The District sends a "get well" card to each injured worker who will be off the job longer than 72 hours.

9. To ensure that risk assessment is included in new account start-ups, the District Safety Coordinator will be successful in this Key Results Area when:

   a. Managers identify special risks in accounts and consider those when accepting the job.

   b. Risk assessment includes the potential for second party liability, i.e., slips and falls when we are cleaning during business hours.

   c. All safety equipment, including warning signs, are on hand at the time the account is started.

   d. Jobs are turned down which are too hazardous, i.e., high rise window cleaning (except for *Your Company Name's* Special Services Division.)

10. To develop a productive District Safety committee, the District Safety Coordinator will be successful in this Key Results Area when:

    a. A safety committee has been established.

    b. Committee members consider safety meetings and safety programs an important part of their jobs.

    c. Recurring monthly safety meetings are scheduled. This means that they are scheduled at the same time on the same day every month, for example the second Friday of each month at 2 PM.

    d. The District Manager chairs the meeting.

    e. Committee member attendance is near 100%.

    f. Accidents and incidents occurring during the month are discussed and practical suggestions are made to prevent reoccurrence.

      g. New MSDS are reviewed and any special hazards are identified.

      h. A special safety topic is highlighted every month.

ORGANIZATIONAL RELATIONSHIPS:

The District Safety Coordinator is supervised by the District Manager or Project Manager for assignments, guidance, evaluation and problem solving. Since there is daily telephone and in-person contact with internal and external customers, a harmonious and cooperative attitude must be maintained.

NOTE:

Job/Position Descriptions are written to give employees and Supervisors information about the job. They are not contracts of any kind. Employees can be reassigned at any time and given other duties within the Corporation. Not all jobs have position descriptions. It is impossible to list each and every duty in a position description and employees are expected to follow the instructions of their Supervisor whether or not those instructions are included in a job description.

JOB AND PERFORMANCE DESCRIPTIONS

LIGHT DUTY SPECIALIST, VACUUM SPECIALIST, RESTROOM SPECIALIST, UTILITY SPECIALIST, FLOOR MACHINE SPECIALIST

All cleaning specialist jobs require the following qualifications

SPECIFIED RESPONSIBILITIES:

1. Perform cleaning duties at a maximum quality level.

2. Perform work within production time budgets and supply budgets.

3. Keep equipment clean and in good operating condition.

4. Follow all safety rules and participate in company's safety program.

5. Project a professional image and maintain good customer and public relations.

6. Adhere to company rules, policies, and operating procedures.

7. Reports to the site supervisor any equipment breakdowns, unsafe conditions, customer complaints and any other problems that may occur.

8. Adhere to tardiness and absenteeism policy.

9. Be able to work schedule as assigned by supervisor at various locations.

JOB AND PERFORMANCE DESCRIPTIONS

LIGHT DUTY SPECIALIST, VACUUM SPECIALIST, RESTROOM SPECIALIST, UTILITY SPECIALIST, FLOOR MACHINE SPECIALIST

All cleaning specialist jobs require the following qualifications

QUALIFICATION REQUIREMENTS:

To perform this successfully, an individual must be able to perform each essential duty satisfactorily. The requirements listed below are representative of the knowledge, skill and/or ability required. Reasonable accommodations may be made to enable individuals with disabilities to perform the essential functions.

Must have dependable transportation or be able to get to the job site scheduled.

LANGUAGE SKILLS:

Ability to read a limited number of two and three syllable words and to recognize similarities and differences between words and between series of numbers. Ability to print and speak simple sentences in English.

REASONING ABILITY:

Ability to apply common-sense understanding to carry out simple one- or two-step instructions. Ability to deal with standardized situations with only occasional or no variables.

JOB AND PERFORMANCE DESCRIPTIONS

LIGHT DUTY SPECIALIST, VACUUM SPECIALIST, RESTROOM SPECIALIST, UTILITY SPECIALIST, FLOOR MACHINE SPECIALIST

All cleaning specialist jobs require the following qualifications

PHYSICAL DEMANDS:

The physical demands described here are representative of those which must be met by an employee to successfully perform the essential functions of the job.

Must be able to perform manual tasks requiring strength and to be in good physical health.

While performing the duties of the job, the employee is regularly required to reach with hands and arms. The employee continually is required to stand, walk, stoop, kneel, crouch and bend. The employee is repetitively required to use hands and fingers, to handle objects and equipment, to push and pull, to climb and balance, and to talk and hear. The employee must repeatedly lift and/or move up to 50 pounds. Specific vision abilities required by this job include close vision, distance vision, color vision, peripheral vision, depth perception, and the ability to adjust focus.

WORK ENVIRONMENT:

The work environment characteristics described here are representative of that an employee encounters while performing the essential functions of this job. Reasonable accommodations may be made to enable individuals with disabilities to perform the essential functions. While performing the duties of this job, the employees occasionally work near moving mechanical parts and are occasionally exposed to toxic or caustic chemicals, risk of electric shock, and vibration. The noise level in the work environment is usually moderate.

While this job description is intended to be an accurate reflection of the job requirements, management reserves the right to modify, add or remove duties from particular jobs and to assign other duties as necessary.

Additional educational resources available from Consultants In Cleaning, LLC.

BOOK(S)

Selling Contract Cleaning Services 101

VIDEO CD'S

Closing the Sale
Components of a Successful Sales Proposal
Prospects You Should Not Pursue
Reducing Turnover
Selling Big on a Small Budget
Selling Strong in Today's Economy
Why Can't They Do It Right?
Why Should Anyone Buy From You?

All of the above items are available at www.consultantsincleaning.com

In addition, Dick can be heard on a free weekly pod cast at www.tripodcast.com

LaVergne, TN USA
15 June 2010
186159LV00007B/3/P